PARENTING
TEENS *in*
STRESSFUL
TIMES

JENNIFER DOTY PhD, CFLE

&

JESSICA PETERSON MSW, LICSW

CFI

An imprint of Cedar Fort, Inc.

Springville, Utah

© 2022 Jennifer Doty and Jessica Peterson
All rights reserved.

No part of this book may be reproduced in any form whatsoever, whether by graphic, visual, electronic, film, microfilm, tape recording, or any other means, without prior written permission of the publisher, except in the case of brief passages embodied in critical reviews and articles.

The opinions and views expressed herein belong solely to the author and do not necessarily represent the opinions or views of Cedar Fort, Inc. Permission for the use of sources, graphics, and photos is also solely the responsibility of the author.

ISBN 13: 978-1-4621-4120-3

Published by CFI, an imprint of Cedar Fort, Inc.
2373 W. 700 S., Springville, UT 84663
Distributed by Cedar Fort, Inc., www.cedarfort.com

Library of Congress Control Number: 2021949091

Cover design by Shawnda T. Craig
Cover design © 2022 Cedar Fort, Inc.
Edited and typeset by Valene Wood

Printed in the United States of America

10 9 8 7 6 5 4 3 2 1

Printed on acid-free paper

Jennifer

To the people who have taught me the most:
my children—Claire, Haven, and Nate.

And to Matthew, my partner-in-crime.

Jessica

To my children: Taylor Waylor, Sarah Bear,
Jamesy Whamsey, Benny Ben, and Lizzie Liz.
Your personalities, talents, spunk, challenges, and
amazingness inspire me to be a better human every
day. I'm glad to be sharing the journey with you.

To my husband: You have endless patience with
my sense of adventure, spontaneity, and passion
for learning. You have my heart.

CONTENTS

PART ❶

Emotional and Relational
Foundations of Resilience

CHAPTER 1

Why Teach Resilience to Teenagers?

Who knew when we started this book a few years back, that we'd finish it in the middle of a worldwide pandemic? Who knew that we'd be raising a generation to rise to unique challenges? Who knew that our kids would all need resilience in a way that hasn't been called for in more than half a century? In a media-saturated world, they've had to spend exponentially more time online, as many have struggled with online schooling. Some are actually thriving away from the everyday pressure of high school, but many more continue to wrestle with issues such as depression, anxiety, bullying, peer pressure, loneliness, questions of faith, and fear about the future.

When our youth face heart-wrenching challenges, as parents, how can we help them find resolve to keep going, deal with life and seek comfort in friends, leaders, and the gospel? How can we help them heal in a world rocked by a pandemic, economic turmoil, and personal challenges? This book explores these questions and provides support to parents who are trying to help their kids to rise above difficult times—in short, we aim to promote resilience.

DEVELOPING RESILIENCE

In engineering, resilience refers to the strength and flexibility of a structure to hold up under a heavy load or a severe disturbance—think about a bridge that doesn't fall apart under high winds or a building that doesn't crack when there's an earthquake.[1] In either example, the structure is challenged, but it holds up often because it is built to be flexible and has the right support. In humans, resilience means being able to hold up under pressure, stress, and challenge.

One of the first studies of resilience began in 1955 on a Hawaiian island and followed at-risk children from before birth into adulthood who had all experienced prenatal stress.[2] Some of the "children of the garden island" had the odds stacked against them—they had birth complications and lived in poverty with unstable parents. As they grew older, most of these high-risk kids were vulnerable to physical challenges, learning problems, behavior issues, mental disorders, and early pregnancy. Still, some seemed to beat the odds—they developed strong relationships, did well in school, and reached their educational and career goals. *What made the difference?* Why were some kids resilient while others weren't? The resilient children tended to have easygoing personalities, and even though they weren't exceptionally talented, they developed the talents they had. They had a close relationship with a parent or found a supportive adult if their parents weren't emotionally available. In their homes, these resilient children had a sense of responsibility—caring for younger children, being a role model, and doing chores. Many of them had a network of support that included friends and mentors, such as a teacher, a leader from church, or a coach. This study of resilient children helped to lay the groundwork to better understand ways that we can all successfully face challenges when our chips are down.

1. Masten, A. S. (2014). Ordinary magic: Resilience in development. New York: Guilford Press.
2. Werner, E. E. (1989). Children of the garden island. Scientific American, *260*, 106–111.

While some social scientists look at severe risks when studying resilience, in this book we think about resilience more broadly.[3] None of us can predict or prevent all the challenges for the teens we care about. In our current high pressure, fast-paced environment, some of them may be more vulnerable than others. Maybe that's because of the genetic risk they carry, traumatic experiences as young children, historical trauma, or a sensitive personality.[4] But since the study of the garden island children, social science has learned much more about how to cultivate resilience. Our first goal is to connect some of these ideas with the doctrines and principles of the gospel that help to prepare our youth to "press forward, feasting upon the word of Christ, and endure to the end."[5]

Sometimes in our Latter-day Saint culture, we think that if we are living the gospel, we won't struggle with mental health. But many of us do—in fact 1 out of 5 of us will likely struggle with a mental disorder at one point in our lives,[6] and since the pandemic, many estimate those numbers are higher. If we don't personally struggle with mental health, it is highly likely that we have a family member or good friend who does. This also means, on a typical Sunday, at least 40 of the people sitting in a typical congregation are currently struggling or may someday struggle with depression, anxiety, an eating disorder, PTSD, or a similar issue. In high poverty areas, those rates are likely to be much higher.[7] We often carry shame when we deal with mental illness or worry that others will blame us for our problems because

---

3. We want to acknowledge that many in our audience have access to resources that poor, underprivileged communities don't have. Here is an opinion piece that underscores the need to address disparities: Hanna-Attisha, M. (2020) I'm sick of asking children to be resilient. Retrieved from https://www.nytimes.com/2020/05/12/opinion/sunday/flint-inequality-race-coronavirus.html.

4. Belsky & Pruess (2009). Beyond diathesis stress: Differential susceptibility to environmental influences. Psychological Bulletin, *135*(6), 885–908.

5. 2 Nephi 31:20

6. This is a conservative estimate: Numbers from the World Health Organization suggest that the United States has the highest prevalence of mental illness, with nearly 1 in 2 people likely to experience mental illness at some point in their lives (Mental Health By the Numbers. *National Alliance on Mental Illness,* Mar. 2021. http://www.nami.org/Learn-More/Mental-Health-By-the-Numbers).

7. Yoshikawa, H., Aber, J. L., & Beardslee, W. R. (2012). The effects of poverty on the mental, emotional, and behavioral health of children and youth: implications for prevention. *American Psychologist, 67*(4), 272–284.

we are not living the gospel the way they think we should. In the last few years, Elder Holland has reminded us that "there should be no more shame in acknowledging [mental illnesses or emotional disorders] than in acknowledging a battle with high blood pressure or the sudden appearance of a malignant tumor."[8] If we can help the teens in our lives to develop skills in resilience early in their lives, these skills will have a lifelong impact.

Over time severe stress often makes us vulnerable to mental health problems. In these pages, we focus on the idea of patient resilience as a reminder that dealing with life's stressors is a learning process that takes time. Rather than a one-time heroic effort when life gets tough, often what we need is the mindset of a marathon runner. In fact, in the New Testament, Paul compares life to a race. He says, "So run, that ye may obtain."[9] This means hours of training, pacing ourselves, and stopping for self-care along the way. In fact, in running a marathon, pushing too hard and too fast out of the gate will tank a runner's time. Paul later advises, "Let us lay aside every weight . . . and let us run with patience the race that is set before us."[10] Every weight—that might include worries about what others think of us or pressure to be involved in multiple extra activities. As adults, we have the benefit of years of experience in deciding what burdens to put down, but many of us are still learning what it means to endure to the end.

Our teenagers, though, don't have the benefit of years of experience. The four years of high school are more than a quarter of their lives—that seems like a long time to endure challenges when you are 13 or 14 and life as a freshman isn't going so well. Teenagers often need help deciding what burdens to put down and how to let go of some of the heavy weight they carry.

CHALLENGES FOR YOUNG PEOPLE TODAY

Even before the pandemic, life was more complex for this generation of teenagers than it has been in the past. The American Psychological

---

8. Holland, J.R. (2013). Like a broken vessel. *General Conference, Oct.*
9. 1 Corinthians 9:24
10. Hebrews 12:1

Association found that teens' stress levels have risen almost to the level of adult stress levels.[11] Our kids are stressed out about time, money, friends and family, and the future. A majority of children in the U.S. will live part of their childhood in a single parent home.[12] The transition to adulthood has become much more stressful. The pressure to get into college has increased, but it's harder to be accepted.[13] The cost of education has increased, but jobs are harder to find, especially jobs that will offset the high cost of education.[14] People used to stick with a career their entire life, but now young people have to be prepared to switch careers multiple times in their lives. It is no wonder that the stress levels of teenagers are approaching adult levels of stress, what one teen called "the overwhelming feeling of being overwhelmed."

Here is a practical example from Jessica, contrasting her experience with her graduate students'. "When I was in graduate school, I lived with my husband. I paid for my education from my work and a scholarship given to me by my employer. Tuition at my graduate school has increased 215%, which is similar to overall increases in the cost of higher education.[13] In an informal survey of my current graduate students over the last several years, nearly half of them lived with or had some financial support of their parents." Forbes looked at student data from LendEDU and found a similar trend—more than

11. Bethune, S. (2012). Teen stress rivals that of adults. American Psychological Association. http://www.apa.org/monitor/2014/04/teen-stress.

12. Tolan, P. (2014). Forward thinking: Preparing our youth for the coming world. *Journal of Research on Adolescence, 24*(3), 411–416.
    See also: 2014 Kids Count Data Book: 2014 State Trends in Child Well-being. *Annie E. Casey Foundation*, 22 July 2014, http://www.aecf.org/resources/the-2014-kids-count-data-book.

13. In 1991, 5/6 students who applied to BYU were accepted; in 2010, 2/3; now acceptance rates are 1/2 (Hafen, Bruce C. and Rex E. Lee. (Jan. 1991). A Conversation about BYU Admissions, *Ensign*. See also Entrance Stats. BYU Enrollment Services, https://enrollment.byu.edu/admissions/entrance-averages).
    Most Latter-day Saint students, however, do not go to a church school. Seminary and institute numbers at a glance. (2017), https://www.churchofjesuschrist.org/study/ensign/2017/08/seminary-and-institute-at-a-glance?lang=eng,
    For a fascinating discussion on why acceptance rates have been declining, read pages 38–41 of Bruni, F. (2015). *Where you go is not who you'll be.* New York: Grand Central Publishing.

14. Baum, S., Ma, J., (2012). Trends in College Pricing, 2012. In: Trends in Higher Education Series. *The College Board.* http://trends.collegeboard.org/sites/default/files/college-pricing-2012-full-report_0.pdf.

half of students received financial help from parents.[15] The cost of education has made financial independence difficult. Those unsupported by parents find themselves racked with debt difficult to resolve—in the same study, more than half of students with debt had a hard time keeping up with daily expenses or finding capital to start a business. Emerging research shows that the accumulation of student loans is related to poor psychological functioning in young adulthood.[16]

Living the gospel may also be stressful for some young people, because it means swimming against the tide of opinions, fashion, and fads. Here's an example from the other author, Jen: "In the weeks before homecoming, my household goes into high-stress mode as the search for a dress begins. Hours and hours go into this process, and usually a lot of tears too. There are very few options in the stores. I once made the mistake of thinking that we might find more modest dresses shopping in Utah, but after hours of searching, we discovered that the dresses were even more picked over than they were in Minnesota. At the end of the night, I saw one mother and daughter in the dressing room evaluating an outfit for modesty. I asked them, 'Where do people find homecoming dresses out here?' The mother explained that there was a boutique where we could find a dress for around $500, but even then, it would probably need modifications! Think about the stress, pressure, and cost of participating in this activity, and that doesn't include the challenge of navigating dates and after parties that go hand in hand with Homecoming. Sometimes, my girls have managed to find a dress at a reasonable cost and a group of friends to go with. Other times, my girls have decided to just cut their losses but have then struggled with feeling lonely and left out when Homecoming weekend rolls around seeing highlights of 'perfect' dates on Facebook and Instagram. These stories lead us back to the question, 'How can we prepare our children to deal with the stress of living in today's world?'"

---

15. Priceonomics. (2017). How much help do millennials get from their parents paying for college? *Forbes.* https://www.forbes.com/sites/priceonomics/2017/05/18/how-much-help-do-millennials-get-from-their-parents-paying-for-college/#7b192d1e7cf5.

16. Walsemann, K. M., Gee, G. C., & Gentile, D. (2015). Sick of our loans: Student borrowing and the mental health of young adults in the United States. *Social Science & Medicine, 124,* 85–93.

AN OVERVIEW OF THIS BOOK

Another goal of this book is to help families and leaders teach coping skills to our youth, encourage them to set healthy boundaries, and help them to get help when needed. Half of teens surveyed report that they don't have good ways to deal with the stress they feel.[17] When a teenager starts to slide into depression, it can be harder to spot than when an adult becomes depressed because some depression symptoms in teenagers are actually different than adult symptoms. How can we recognize early on if our kids need help dealing with depression or another emotional challenge? What skills do we need to practice as parents to model healthy coping and support our kids? How do we help them with living the gospel when it means being different from their peers? How do we prepare our missionaries to be away from home in a new culture? How do we help a missionary who has come home early?

These are not easy questions. And we don't pretend to have all the answers. In fact, maybe this is a good time to admit that writing this book has sometimes made us both a bit queasy, knowing that anyone who looks closely at our lives will be able to see mistakes that we have made personally, professionally, and as parents. Both of us have worked with teenagers for years, both in our professions and in the church, and both of us have had the humbling experience of being parents of teenagers. Some of the answers to these questions seem more difficult and nuanced now that we wrestle with them on a daily basis. But because of our professional experiences, Jen as an adolescent health researcher and Jessica as a therapist, we feel like we have some practical insights to share.

Over 20 years ago, Jen's career in youth development and family science began as a shift supervisor at an adolescent treatment center for girls with serious mental health challenges. She began to see how important family changes were to supporting the individual changes girls made in treatment as they transitioned back home, and she decided to go back to school to learn more. After getting a master's degree, she taught human development and family policy courses for several years as a part-time adjunct professor. Once her kids were in

---

17. Are Teens Adopting Adults' Stress Habits? *American Psychological Association* (2014), http://www.apa.org/news/press/releases/stress/2013/teen-stress.aspx.

school, her family moved to Minnesota, so she could go back to school again and get a PhD in Family Science. She worked as a researcher of adolescent health in the Pediatrics department at the University of Minnesota, and now as an assistant professor of youth development and prevention at the University of Florida. Her research focuses on strengthening the parent-adolescent relationship to improve adolescent health outcomes. She has worked with youth for years at girls' camp and in the Young Women program, and she spent four years as an early morning seminary teacher.

Jessica has been a licensed clinical social worker for over 20 years, working in community and clinical settings. She started as a child welfare worker in Utah, and then she went back to school to get a master's in social work. She was a therapist at LDS Social Services for 11 years in Pennsylvania, Ohio, and Minnesota. In that capacity, she worked with teenagers, parents, missionaries, and mission presidents. She's worked in free clinics, an alternative high school, a hospital, and a private practice—her wide range of experience has provided perspective on different challenges families of teenagers face today. She has also taught classes in social work, including clinical training, at St. Catherine University and the University of St. Thomas in St. Paul Minnesota. Recently, Jessica has served in ward and stake Young Women programs.

The gospel is the foundational framework of this book, and we draw from the scriptures for principles and stories that illustrate ways to strengthen resilience. We also hope to provide practical information and relationship tools that we have learned from research, therapy, and our personal experience working with teenagers.

Chapters 2 & 3: We start by building emotional awareness and exploring the role of negative and positive emotions in our everyday lives. When we are striving to live the gospel, sometimes we get caught up in the idea that we should never feel overwhelmed with fear, anger, or hopelessness . . . but challenging emotions are *given* to us by our Creator. In chapter 2, we focus on understanding them and finding healthy ways to cope with them, which is key to our happiness in the long run. In chapter 3, we also share research on ways to cultivate positive emotions while being authentic about developing the full range of emotions we experience.

Chapter 4, 5, & 6: The next three chapters focus on parenting more directly, outlining considerations for working with teenagers and getting professional help. As parents, we get a lot of parenting information and support when our children are little, but raising teenagers comes with new challenges. Chapter 4 addresses issues that are common during teenage years: building a strong relationship, avoiding power struggles, and setting healthy limits. In chapter 5, we address the concept of balance—emotional health and patient parenting are also about recognizing when to keep boundaries and when to push forward. In Chapter 6, we focus on promoting spirituality in our youth. We look at strategies for encouraging youth to build a spiritual foundation. Then we take on a delicate question: How do we balance the "shoulds" of living the gospel as a member of the Church of Jesus Christ against mental health needs?

Chapters 7 & 8: The next two chapters focus on intentionally practicing the two great commandments as parents: love the Lord thy God and love your neighbor as yourself. We offer practical suggestions for parents and teenagers that help us to put these commandments into practice in our busy, often hectic lives. Chapter 7 focuses on themes of mindfulness in our worship—the ideas of standing still, sincere prayer, and connecting to God in nature. Then, in Chapter 8, we consider how self-compassion is foundational to loving others. Without self-compassion, we have a difficult time connecting with other people. This section concludes with a discussion in Chapter 8 about loving others by trying to understand their "intents of the heart."

This book is informed by what we have learned along our journey—which admittedly is ongoing. A few years back, our stake president talked about when Christ's disciples woke Him up because of a fierce storm on the Sea of Galilee. He calmed the seas—not necessarily because the storm was bothering Him, but because the disciples asked Him to. But the Lord doesn't take away our personal storms most of the time. In fact, it was our stake president's opinion that the Lord loves a good storm—because He knows that we can learn and grow from being challenged. While there are some emotional storms that we can't prepare for, gospel principles can help us build resilience to get through the storms of life, strengthen our mental health, and thrive in the gospel.

CHAPTER 2

Understanding Uncomfortable Emotions

Imagine that you are one of the children of Israel, and you have just left Egypt because Moses convinced Pharaoh to let you go. In the last few weeks, you have witnessed a series of incredible miracles. The Israelites have been spared ten plagues, including the Passover where the firstborn son of every family was saved. How would you feel as you set out into the wilderness? You might feel gratitude, invigorated by your freedom, maybe a bit of nervousness because you are completely out of your comfort zone. But every day you wake up, and God leads you in a pillar of cloud, and at night He stands watch in a pillar of fire.[1]

With these experiences and protections, you have grown to respect Moses as a leader and learned to trust the God of Israel. When God tells Moses to camp by the edge of the sea, you pitch your tent without questioning. But now, imagine looking out across the distant desert horizon. The horizon looks hazy, and you start to see dust clouds. Then, six-hundred chariots come into view, and the entire Egyptian army is coming your direction. How would you feel now? The account says, "They were sore afraid." They turned on the sarcasm and complained

---

1. Exodus 12–13

bitterly to Moses, "Because there were no graves in Egypt, hast thou taken us away to die in the wilderness?"[2]

The response of the Israelites is a classic fight-or-flight response. Take one of your hands and touch the back of your head at the nape of your neck. You can't feel it, but in front of your hand is a small almond-shaped structure called the amygdala. The amygdala is the danger detection center of the brain.[3] As fear floods the brain, the amygdala is firing off messages preparing the body to respond. Blood is siphoned away from the planning and strategy part of the brain, and extra blood is sent to the extremities. In short, the arms and legs are prepared to run, punch, and kick. But pay attention to how Moses responds: "Fear ye not, stand still, and see the salvation of the Lord."[4] Moses gives great advice for coping with negative emotions, and we are going to discuss Moses' directives further. But before we do, let's consider biological systems of fear and other negative emotions.

FEELING FEAR AND STRESS

To understand fear and our stress response system, it's helpful to know a little bit about how our brain works. The amygdala is like the reptilian brain.[5] Have you ever seen a lizard running around? Every few seconds they startle as if they were looking for danger. Unlike lizards, we have a much more complex brain that includes the prefrontal cortex, the part of your brain right behind your forehead. This is the executive thinking center of the brain, responsible for brainstorming solutions, strategizing, and planning for the future. Normally the prefrontal cortex keeps our fears in check by rationalizing, creating positive and neutralizing self-talk, and calming ourselves down.

---

2. Exodus 14:10–11
3. Hanson, R. (2009). *Buddha's brain: The practical neuroscience of happiness, love, and wisdom*. Oakland, CA: New Harbinger Publications.
4. Exodus 14:13
5. The comparison of the amygdala is a useful metaphor, but strictly speaking, the limbic system which the amygdala is a part of is only found in mammals. The job description of the amygdala does include fear, but also other strong reactions (Allen, Stephanie W, (2012). Clearing up confusion: The amygdala is not the same as the reptile brain & it's probably not reserved for fear. *Brains on Purpose*, http://westallen. typepad.com/brains_on_purpose/2012/01/clearing-up-confusion.html).

When we are really afraid, basically, the brain flips its lid and the amygdala takes over. Fear itself is not a bad thing, though. In fact, our Savior, Jehovah, who is the Creator of the universe and the designer of the incredible systems in our bodies, gave us the fear system in our brains. Fear is a God-given gift that works to protect us in dangerous situations and helps keep us on task. For example, a certain amount of anxiety helps us to be on time to school or meetings and get homework turned in. You may wear a seat belt because of fear of an accident or go the speed limit because you are afraid of getting a ticket. However, problems arise when fear is constant and never takes a break. Fight-or-flight mode may have been useful thousands of years ago if you had to kill a lion, but in today's modern world it can be stressful to always have the amygdala firing off. In fact, science has linked this kind of stress to long-term systemic inflammation and health problems.[6]

Having the reptilian brain take over isn't so helpful when we need to problem-solve. We literally can't think straight when fear takes over, and it's hard to come up with solutions to the problem at hand.[7] Most of us have been taught that fear doesn't come from God[8]—we suspect that this teaching refers to inhibiting, stressful, overwhelming fear rather than the fear that keeps us safe on a daily basis. If we are continually stressed out, we are ready to fight or run constantly. Today, if a teen is sitting all day in a classroom, she can't necessarily fight or run, and that energy might get directed into irritation or anger. And she can't run away from her problems, but instead she might start avoiding everyone by holing up in her bedroom for hours. Other teenagers might become obsessed with social media, binge watch TV series, or over-involve themselves to avoid interpersonal relationships. If you notice increased irritation and avoidance in your teenager, it might be a red flag that he is feeling emotionally overwhelmed.

In the meantime, here's an example from the home front of kids feeling emotionally overwhelmed. When Jen's kids were younger, her sister-in-law Amber mentioned that her daughter came home from

---

6. Segerstrom, S. C., & Miller, G. E. (2004). Psychological stress and the human immune system: a meta-analytic study of 30 years of inquiry. *Psychological bulletin, 130*(4), 601–630.
7. Kahneman, D. (2011). *Thinking, fast and slow*. Macmillan.
8. 2 Timothy 1:7

school one day in a foul mood and started incessantly picking on her sister. She started to reprimand her, but then her daughter broke down in tears and told her about the horrible day she had at school. A few weeks later Jen had the same experience. Her daughter came home and started laying into her siblings. Remembering Amber's experience, she asked, "Are you ok? You're not acting like yourself—did something happen at school?" Sure enough, she had problems with some kids at school during lunch that day. Irritation can be a signal that something more is going on. Having insight into what is happening in our kids' lives and asking good questions during crucial moments can bring you closer to your children.

Not surprisingly, our Creator has given us some biological tools to deal with fear and stress. Some stress in moderation can actually be a good thing. If we know that tomorrow is going to be a tough day, as we sleep our body gets ready for that. About 30 minutes after we wake up, we get an extra burst of the hormone cortisol, and it prepares us for daily stressors: "All right—I'm ready for this crazy day." But when this happens every day—for weeks or months, or even years, it becomes a problem because our bodies can't maintain that level of energy and have to readjust. We are less likely to get that burst of cortisol. Basically, research has shown that when we get really burnt out or depressed, we feel flat inside, in part because we are no longer getting the same shot of cortisol in the mornings.[9] That flat feeling is another red flag, and if it lasts for several weeks, we might need some help to deal with depression, anxiety, or stress. With that short lesson in biology as background, we turn to understanding our negative emotions.

FEELING SADNESS & HOPELESSNESS

Research shows that anxiety and depression have a number of causes including biology, exposure to trauma, and sustained stress over time. Additionally, clinical anxiety, which often requires treatment to overcome, may be fed by fear that has gone out of control, and depression

---

9. Chida, Y., & Steptoe, A. (2009). Cortisol awakening response and psychosocial factors: a systematic review and meta-analysis. *Biological psychology*, *80*(3), 265–278.

may be fed by a deep and enduring sense of sadness. In the wake of the COVID-19 pandemic, for example, adolescents are reporting record-high stress levels and elevated depression,[10] which is not surprising since the adults around them are living with sustained stress as well.[11] In addition, if your child has experienced complex trauma, for example physical violence, sexual abuse, or other emotional trauma, they will likely need additional mental health treatment.

In our everyday lives, however, the emotion of sadness has an important role to play in giving us a balanced perspective and helping us get support. The movie *Inside Out* is a great example of this.[12] In this story, we meet the personified emotions of a little girl named Riley who has had to move away from Minnesota to California with her family. The character Joy is frustrated with the character Sadness who says things like, "Crying helps me slow down and obsess over the weight of life's problems." And, "I'm too sad to walk. Just give me a few hours." At one point, Joy draws a circle and instructs Sadness to stay in the circle. In our lives, most of us have been there—trying to avoid feeling sad. Who wants a stuffy nose and puffy eyes, right? Even the people around us don't want us to feel sad. At some point, you've probably been told some version of "Chin up," "It was probably for the best," or "It will be alright."

By the end of the movie, though, the character Joy realized that the emotion of sadness activated her support system and helped her get help from the people who love her. For a while Riley hardened her heart and wanted to run away, but when she got in touch with her sadness, she went to her parents to get some help. Another interesting thing happened in the movie—at the beginning of the movie, all of her memories were stored in brightly colored globes full of joy, joy, joy. But then sadness touched them, and they all turned blue. By the

---

10. American Psychological Association. (2020). Stress in America 2020: A national mental health crisis. https://www.apa.org/news/press/releases/stress/2020/report-october.

11. Patrick, S. W., Henkhaus, L. E., Zickafoose, J. S., Lovell, K., Halvorson, A., Loch, S., Letterie, M., & Davis, M. M. (2020). Well-being of parents and children during the COVID-19 pandemic: A national survey. *Pediatrics, 146*(4), e2020016824. https://doi.org/10.1542/peds.2020-016824.

12. Rivera, J. (Producer), & Docter, Pt. (Director). 2015. *Inside Out* [Motion picture]. United States: Disney.

end of the movie, the memories were multi-colored, richer and more realistic. It can be exhausting to be constantly curbing our sadness and not allowing ourselves the full range of emotions.

In cognitive terms, this can be considered changing black and white thinking to gray thinking. Imagine for a moment that your child just failed an algebra test. He studied, prepared, and felt ready to take it. He didn't just fail; the test obliterated him—23 out of 100 points. He comes home and tells you, "I'm the dumbest kid in the class. I can't do this anymore. Make room for me in the basement because the chances of me getting into college just ended." When you hear this, do you agree, join him in his negative thinking and start clearing your clutter to make room for a lifelong roommate? Probably not! If you are reading this book, you probably want to figure out how to help your child. Instead, the mistake you and I often make is that we say: "That just isn't true. You are smart, capable, amazing, and you are going to get into Harvard!" (Okay, maybe you don't go that far.) You are trying to help, but your child can't hear you. They want to, but the most recent evidence they have is that they are a failure. The evidence is blinding them to all reason. It's actually more helpful at this point if you acknowledge the failure. "That stinks. I can tell you are upset, and I know you really wanted to do well. Two weeks ago you nailed that test in Algebra, and this one didn't go the way you planned." A response like this validates their feelings. It draws on specific evidence, and it doesn't provide advice (did you talk to the teacher, study hard enough, get enough sleep etc.). There is time for advice on changing future outcomes later. Helping them process the emotion of the event using balanced thinking will help them to problem solve doing better next time.

Another thing we can do to set a good example for our teenagers is to be honest with our emotions and share when we feel sad. Yes, the gospel is geared toward maximizing our happiness, but God also gave us the capacity to have a full range of emotions. Brené Brown, a researcher who studies vulnerability and shame, has studied individuals who are "wholehearted." She noticed that if someone is using the full capacity of his heart, he allows himself to feel the whole spectrum of emotions.[13] Brown found that these individuals lean into their vulnerability, and in doing so, find genuine connections with other people. We highly recommend her TED talk "The Power of Vulnerability."

FEELING ANGER

Anger is sometimes referred to as a secondary emotion because it often masks emotional pain or vulnerability. This is essentially a strategy of "the best defense is a good offense." At times, anger can be a primary emotion in the face of danger—the first emotion activated by a biological fight response.[14] In this respect, it can be protective in some situations, like when our ancestors saw a bear stalking their young and started waving their arms and yelling to scare the bear off.

In Latter-day Saint culture, we often think of anger as "bad." Certainly, we are warned against contention in 3 Nephi 11:29, but is contention the same thing as anger? The word "contend" implies an element of competition—if you contend with someone, there is a winner and a loser. It is not the feeling but what we do with the feeling that can be a problem. If we start waving our arms and yelling at our teenagers, they will definitely want to stay away from us. Emotional distance and loneliness are linked to poor mental health in young people, such as depression, anxiety, cutting, bullying, or drinking.[15] On the other hand, connections with adults—parents, teachers, youth leaders, and mentors—help protect youth from negative outcomes. For example, study after study shows that kids who have strong, healthy connections with adults are less likely to participate in

---

13. Brown, B. (2012). *Daring greatly: How the courage to be vulnerable transforms the way we live, love, parent, and lead.* New York, N.Y. : Gotham Books.

14. Diamond, S. (2009). The Primacy of Anger Problems. https://www.psychologytoday.com/blog/evil-deeds/200901/the-primacy-anger-problems

15. Jones, A. C., Schinka, K. C., van Dulmen, M. H., Bossarte, R. M., & Swahn, M. H. (2011). Changes in loneliness during middle childhood predict risk for adolescent suicidality indirectly through mental health problems. *Journal of Clinical Child & Adolescent Psychology, 40*(6), 818–824. See also, The Crisis of Connection for Boys with Niobe Way (2017), https://www.youtube.com/watch?v=7ScAvJ0KiyU.

risky behaviors like drinking, skipping school, or bullying.[16] So how do we stay connected when we are downright angry at our kids?

When we are not in immediate danger, it can be a useful exercise to notice our anger and take a time-out to think about why we are angry. Maybe we are embarrassed by our teens' behavior in public. Maybe we are hurt by the inattention that family members give to picking up their stuff and the implication that Mom is the family maid who cleans up after everyone. Maybe we are feeling anxious about a job interview or exhausted after a family reunion. In those situations, once we are calm, it usually pays off to express the real emotion. Sometimes we need to wait for the right moment to share how we're feeling. For example, teenagers, nocturnal creatures that they are, may be open to talking late at night—some of the best conversations parents have with teens is around midnight when they get home from hanging out with friends. Regardless of the time of the conversation, when understanding between two people happens, there are two winners.

In contrast, stuffing anger—or other emotions—deep down can lead to resentment boiling below the surface. In the Doty house, they've kept the following quote hung on our wall since the day they got married: "In essentials unity, in non-essentials liberty, and in all things charity." Over the years, it has been a useful guideline Jen has used to decide when to share anger or frustration. If something bothers her, she tries to decide if it is essential or non-essential. If she thinks that the problem is non-essential, she puts it on a shelf and waits for a few days. Most of the time, the frustration subsides, and she forgets about it. But if she feels angry or frustrated a few days later, then she knows that she has to talk with the family member about the issue that got under her skin. In her own words, here's an example: "We have a new puppy in our house, a dark-haired boxer named Kevin. Last summer, my husband Matthew wanted to make sure that the puppy got the highest quality dog food. I joked with the kids that

---

16. Sieving, R. E., McRee, A. L., McMorris, B. J., Shlafer, R. J., Gower, A. L., Kapa, H. M., Beckman, K. J., Doty, J. L., Plowman, S. L., Resnick, M. D. (in press). Youth-adult connectedness: A key protective factor for adolescent health. *American Journal of Preventive Medicine.*

Bowes, L., Maughan, B., Caspi, A., Moffitt, T.E., Arseneault, L. (2010) Families promote emotional and behavioural resilience to bullying: Evidence of an environmental effect. *Journal of Child Psychology and Psychiatry. 51*(7), 809–817.

Kevin got the good stuff, but I was actually a bit annoyed and snippy on an occasion or two. When Matthew and I talked about it, I realized that my real concern was keeping our budget, especially with our kids' college and missions around the corner. So we ended up compromising—Costco dog food to the rescue!"

One book that applies this principle to parenting is "The Explosive Child."[17] It describes creating three virtual baskets of parenting priorities. Basket A is your essential non-negotiable things. These are said to be the things you are willing to engage in high conflict over (think meltdown worthy). It's important Basket A is very limited. Basket B includes high-priority things you would like your child to do but might not be worth a meltdown or power struggle. As you prioritize things that belong in Basket B, you are willing to negotiate and hear your teen's viewpoint and are willing to change. Basket C includes the things you hope your child will do but are not your highest priority. Everyone's baskets look different in parenting as some of us stress different things.

Unity between parents is critical, though. It's also important to back up other parents' choices with their children and not impose your Basket A on another family. When we back each other up, we both win. When you find friends who back up your parenting, you both parent better. The exception to this principle is abuse. The Church is clear in their message that it does not condone any form of abuse. If you are struggling with being abusive toward your spouse or children, please get professional help. If you are aware of a child being abused, find a way to assist that child. We cannot tolerate uncontrolled anger when a child's life is at stake.

FEELING SHAME

Shame can hinder our ability to connect with our children. Dr. Brené Brown defines shame as, "the intensely painful feeling or experience of believing that we are flawed and therefore unworthy of love and

---

17. Greene, R. W. (2014). The explosive child: a new approach for understanding and parenting easily frustrated, chronically inflexible children. Revised and updated. New York: Harper.

belonging—something we've experienced, done, or failed to do makes us unworthy of connection."[18] In her research, she found that when she asked people about connection to other people, what she heard instead were stories of shame.

Brown distinguishes between shame and guilt. Shame attacks our very self-worth, our sense of who we are as individuals, but guilt is focused on feeling bad about something we've done. Shame is destructive self-loathing, and the research shows that it is associated with poor health outcomes such as eating disorders, drinking, depression, and bullying.[19] In contrast, guilt that can prompt change connects us to other people and is related to self-esteem and empathy.[20] One researcher noted that guilt was linked to "a tendency to repair."[21] Shame is a favorite tool of the adversary, but guilt is tied to repentance, and an honest effort to change is the very heart of the gospel of Jesus Christ.

Looking at the word repentance in the original languages of the Old Testament and New Testament invites us to focus on the idea of healthy change rather than shame. In Hebrew, the word *teshuvah* is often translated as "repentance" in the Old Testament, but the two words have different meanings. *Teshuvah* means to turn back or return with Jehovah's help, implying that relying on Jehovah is an important part of this process.[22] President Nelson taught, "The

18. Brown, B. (2012). *Daring greatly: How the courage to be vulnerable transforms the way we live, love, parent, and lead*. New York, N.Y.: Gotham Books, 79.

19. Ahmed, E., & Braithwaite, V. (2006). Forgiveness, reconciliation, and shame: Three key variables in reducing school bullying. *Journal of Social Issues, 62*(2), 347-370.
Brown, B. (2012). *Daring greatly: How the courage to be vulnerable transforms the way we live, love, parent, and lead*. New York, N.Y.: Gotham Books.

20. Carnì, S., Petrocchi, N., Del Miglio, C., Mancini, F., & Couyoumdjian, A. (2013). Intrapsychic and interpersonal guilt: a critical review of the recent literature. *Cognitive processing, 14*(4), 333–346.
Kim, S., Thibodeau, R., Jorgensen, R., & Hinshaw, Stephen P. (2011). Shame, Guilt, and Depressive Symptoms: A Meta-Analytic Review. *Psychological Bulletin, 137*(1), 68–96.
Researchers also point out that guilt can be harmful if people take on guilt that is not justified by the situation or live with unresolved "floating" guilt for a situation like divorce.

21. Pivetti, M., Camodeca, M., & Rapino, M. (2016). Shame, guilt, and anger: Their cognitive, physiological, and behavioral correlates. *Current Psychology, 35*(4), 690–699.

22. Nibley, H. (July, 1990). The Atonement of Jesus Christ, part 1. *Ensign.*

word for *repentance* in the Greek New Testament is *metanoeo.* The prefix *meta-* means 'change.' The suffix *-noeo* is related to Greek words that mean 'mind,' 'knowledge,' 'spirit,' and 'breath.' Thus, when Jesus asks you and me to 'repent,' He is inviting us to change our mind, our knowledge, our spirit—even the way we breathe."[23] This idea is much more in line with Alma's question, "Have you received a mighty change in your hearts?"[24]

We all struggle with shame, though. Throughout the scriptures, we see examples of prophets who felt unworthy. When Isaiah is called to be a prophet, he responds, "Woe is me! For I am undone; because I am a man of unclean lips."[25] When Peter lifts his nets and sees the miracle of them bursting with fish after a luckless day of hard work, he falls down before Christ and says, "Depart from me; for I am a sinful man."[26] Even Nephi who seems so strong, asks, "Why should my heart weep and my soul linger in the valley of sorrow, and my flesh waste away, and my strength slacken because of mine afflictions? And why should I yield to sin because of my flesh? . . . Why am I angry because of mine enemy?"[27] In each of these examples, the prophet didn't stay mired in shame and self-loathing, but instead leveraged the feeling of guilt and accepted the invitation to change and follow a new path.

When it comes to teenagers, one of the best things we can do is set an example of becoming "shame resilient." There are so many times when we feel shame because we don't live up to some cultural pressures—women in particular can feel a lot of shame about not being the perfect mom. Those of us who stay home feel like we need to be contributing to the family finances; those of us who work feel like we are dropping the ball on volunteering, callings, and monitoring homework. Moms with a lot of kids might feel judged by others at church, and on the other hand, moms with just one or two kids might feel just as judged. Women who want to have children may feel left out or hurt by thoughtless comments. When kids struggle, we feel

23. Nelson, R. M. (2019). We can do better and be better. General Conference, Apr.
24. Alma 5:14
25. Isaiah 6:5
26. Luke 5:8
27. 2 Nephi 4: 26–27

the personal responsibility of their struggles, even when we know that agency, mistakes, and struggle are all part of the process of learning. Perhaps because of our desire to nurture, we often equate our self-worth with our perceived success as a mother, and shame always attacks our sense of self.

Several years ago, Elder Neal A. Maxwell gave a great talk on helping us overcome the feelings of inadequacy called "Not Withstanding My Weaknesses."[28] He said, "The first thing to be said of this feeling of inadequacy is that it is normal. . . . Following celestial road signs while in telestial traffic jams is not easy, especially when we are not just moving next door—or even across town." Elder Maxwell answered that despair of never feeling good enough with comfort and understanding. Brené Brown also outlined some practical steps to shame resilience:

- Recognizing when shame is triggered—our heart might start pounding, our cheeks might flush.
- Taking a critical look at why we feel shame—is this something we should change or is this a cultural pressure like valuing white teeth and expensive cars?
- Sharing our story with "someone who has earned the right to hear it"—in other words, talking to someone who knows us well and who we can trust to see our whole self can defuse the feeling of shame.
- Because shame thrives when it is hidden, making a regular practice of speaking about our shame to those we are close to helps us keep it in check.[29]

Resisting shame can help us to develop empathy and connect us to other people. We may need to resist shame as part of the repentance process—perhaps this is why talking to someone that we can trust is often an important step in repenting. But notice that often we feel shame because we are comparing ourselves to a cultural standard (or a celestial standard in a telestial world); we feel like we are falling short

---

28. Elder Maxwell. (1976). Not Withstanding My Weakness. General Conference, Oct. See also, Elder Cornish. (2016). Am I good enough? Will I make it? General Conference, Oct.
29. Brown, B. (2012). *Daring greatly: How the courage to be vulnerable transforms the way we live, love, parent, and lead.* New York, N.Y.: Gotham Books.

of expectations. Getting those feelings of shame out into the open is also an important step in resisting shame, and learning to defuse a sense of shame is critical to helping our teenagers learn to do the same.

Teenagers are at a particularly vulnerable age when it comes to shame, because they are often highly self-conscious. Teens may feel a sense of shame not having the latest technology, being overweight, or when someone says "we've missed you" after they have missed a few church activities. When our kids feel deeply unworthy, unpopular, or embarrassed, we can take care to not shame them further. One little guy in first grade was struggling to do a math problem one day. The teacher commented to him in front of the class, "You should never become an accountant!" When he was in high school, he took career tests, and accountant came out on top as one of the best matches for him, but he never even considered it. Today, years later, he speculates that the one negative, public comment from a teacher made a difference in his career choice. Other examples of shaming could be comparing your child to other children in your ward or home or teasing a youth when they show up for an event after months of inactivity.

Instead of shaming or even teasing our youth, we need to practice listening, expressing empathy, and reflecting back to them their intrinsic worth. Watch your son or daughter the next time they get ready to go somewhere. Some youth who are vulnerable to concern about their looks can focus on their clothes, acne, hair, makeup, etc. If your daughter is dressed to kill one day, it may be that she is struggling inside. To parents, a high fashion day may be a signal to check in, see how she is doing, or give her a hug. Following a social interaction, teens may obsess about something they said or didn't say. Sometimes just talking through this with a friend or parent they trust can help them get perspective.

NEGATIVE SPIRALS

Sometimes our teens have a negative thought that leads to another negative thought, that leads to another. For example, if your teen wakes up tired after staying up late studying for a physics test, her first thought might be "I'm going to fail this test." The next thought follows quickly: "If I fail the test, I'm going to fail the class." Then: "If I fail the class, I am not going to graduate." Followed by: "If I don't graduate, I'm never going to college, and I'll never get a job." Then, "I'm going to live with my parents forever, I'll never get married, and I'll die alone and miserable." The progression goes from "I'm tired" to "I'm going to die alone." Negative spirals can happen quickly in an anxiety-driven brain, and this hampers our ability to think rationally.

Thought spirals are often reinforced by pressure. This is a list of external pressures generated by teens during a recent workshop, which is not all inclusive: parents (during 6 presentations, teens almost always listed parents first), friends, coaches, teachers, ACTs, expectations, college applications, sports, performance expectations, relationship issues, seminary, grades, health, and the future. We can help youth with spirals by guiding them to slow down their thinking. Forcing anyone to do an exercise like this is not helpful, but if they are open to it, you can help them map their thoughts on paper. The point of a mind map is not to fix their thoughts but to help you to see where they are coming from.

In Jessica's clinical practice, at times parents are eager to "fix things" and "make a child feel better." She says, "Even with my own children, I often long for the days when chocolate milk and a band aid made the world right again." But most of us, even adults, would prefer to feel heard. A good rule of thumb is to ask, "Would you like me to provide you support or are you looking for advice?" Negative spirals are more likely when we are exhausted emotionally or physically. Teaching our kids the importance of sleep, exercise, and an occasional mental health day may make a huge difference in their ability to cope. We discuss the importance of self-care further in Chapter 8.

PAYING ATTENTION TO THE CONDITION OF OUR HEARTS

We started this chapter with the story of Moses and the children of Israel escaping from Egypt only to be pursued by Pharaoh's army. One of the problems they had with Pharaoh over and over again was that he didn't keep his word. The King James Version of the Old Testament reports that the Lord repeatedly says, "And I will harden Pharoah's heart," but the Joseph Smith Translation says, "And Pharaoh hardened his heart."[30] This is an important distinction because it implies that we have some responsibility for the condition of our hearts. When we feel any uncomfortable emotions of fear, sadness, hopelessness, anger, shame, guilt, resentment, hurt, or rejection, paying attention to the feeling and what it is telling us is important. Only then can we consciously make choices about how to handle that emotion. Remember how Moses responded to the Israelites? "Fear not, stand still, and see the salvation of the Lord." Although fear and other uncomfortable emotions are an important part of being wholehearted, we don't believe that God wants us to stay stuck in a dark place where those emotions reign.

Understanding negative emotions is the first step to diffusing them. For years Jen had been going to school with marriage and family therapists, but it wasn't until one of her kids was in crisis that she stepped into the office for therapy herself. All of the books and theories she had studied for years couldn't prepare her for the feeling of vulnerability sitting on that couch. Her heart was racing, and her palms were sweaty. She wondered, "Will I be judged as a parent? Will I be blamed for my child's problems? Will they see my faith as the problem?" It took time, but as she approached those sessions prayerfully and humbly, she learned to trust the therapeutic relationship and found value in working through challenges sitting on that couch. Managing negative emotions and communication doesn't cure relationships, but it does help families to get "unstuck" when life is intense.

Working through negative emotions is only one side of the equation, though. To have joy and thrive in family life, we need to actively build experiences we enjoy together into our relationships.[31] Cultivating positive emotions is also a key part of the gospel, and the next chapter discusses some of the biological mechanisms related to positive emotions and how "standing still" and recognizing "the salvation of the Lord" are important practices to help us feel joy, happiness, and other positive emotions.

---

30. Exodus 14:13–14; Exodus 14:8, JST
31. O'Neil, Sarah Crane (2017). Make intentional choices to connect with your family. *The Gottman Institute,* https://www.gottman.com/blog/make-intentional-choices-connect-family/.

CHAPTER ❸

Cultivating Positive Emotions

In the midst of their fear and anxiety, Moses assured the children of Israel, "The Lord shall fight for you, and ye shall *hold your peace*" (italics added).[1] That is an interesting phrase—hold your peace—how do we cultivate peace and hold onto it in the middle of challenges or crises? When we are stressed, when we are irritated with everyone around us, and may be complaining just as bitterly as those Israelites, our Savior is still there. He is still willing to give us peace, perspective, and joy. He knows our physical reactions to stress—after all, He is the designer of our neural circuitry. If anyone understands, He does. Still, Moses's command "hold your peace" implies that we have to make an effort to hold onto peace. In fact, the scriptures are full of these types of commands:

- "Be still, and know that I am God." (Psalm 46:10)
- "Fear not: for behold, I bring unto you good tidings of great joy." (Luke 2:10)
- "Look unto me in every thought; doubt not, fear not." (D&C 6:36)
- "Peace, be still." (Mark 4:39)

---

1. Exodus 14:14

A scripture in the Doctrine and Covenants tells us that Moses "brought the children of Israel through the Red Sea on dry ground" by the power of the Holy Ghost.[2] Do you remember that lesson on revelation? The Lord had offered Oliver Cowdery a chance to translate the Book of Mormon, and he was anxious to receive revelation. In Doctrine and Covenants 8, the Lord gave him guidance, and in the process, taught a powerful principle about revelation: "I will tell you in your mind and in your heart, by the power of the Holy Ghost, which shall come upon you and which shall dwell in your heart."[3] So how do we access the same power that Moses did when he parted the Red Sea? How do we follow Moses's advice to hold our peace rather than hardening our hearts? By the power of the Holy Ghost. The Lord went on and told Oliver, "This is thy gift; apply unto it."[4] In other words, we need to patiently practice using the gift of the Holy Ghost and applying revelation in our lives.

When Jen was a little girl, her dad taught her one of his favorite scriptures about peace. It comes from John 14, when the Savior was preparing His disciples to carry on without Him. He taught them about the Holy Ghost, the Comforter, and said, "Peace I leave you, my peace I give unto you: not as the world giveth, give I unto you. Let not your heart be troubled, neither let it be afraid."[5] Again in this verse, the Holy Ghost offers our hearts emotional protection through peace. And another scripture in Galatians teaches us that the fruits of the Spirit are "love, joy, peace, longsuffering, gentleness, goodness, faith, meekness, [and] temperance."[6] These scriptures imply that the Spirit helps us to cultivate positive emotions in our everyday lives and that these qualities can protect us not only spiritually, but also emotionally. In the sections that follow, we explore some of the practical benefits of positive emotions, and then in the next chapters we identify practices that help us to cultivate positive emotions.

---

2. D&C 8:3
3. D&C 8:2
4. D&C 8:4
5. John 14:27
6. Galatians 5:22–23

THE SOCIAL AND EMOTIONAL EFFECTS OF POSITIVE EMOTIONS

In comparison to ancient scriptures, psychological research is relatively new on the human timeline. A search of some of the "best books" in psychology and learning "by study and also by faith"[7] can help us understand, though, how positive emotions can have a long-term impact in our lives. In the gospel, we often consider this from a spiritual perspective, and in this chapter, we'd like to connect social, emotional, and biological perspectives to the spiritual framework that we already have in place. For over a hundred years, psychologists have studied negative emotions like fear and anger, and we know from study after study that they help us to avoid danger in the short term. In other words, we are hardwired to feel these emotions because they help us escape danger, like lions, tigers, and bears. But from a research perspective, we are just starting to learn about the effects of positive emotions.

From what we understand, positive emotions build long-term resources to help us survive and thrive over time. A psychologist named Barbara Frederickson started to notice the connections between positive emotions and well-being—she connected her ideas to research and presented the broaden-and-build theory.[8] In this theory, Frederickson demonstrates two ways positive emotions work.

First, positive emotions broaden or expand our creative thinking. Frederickson had participants watch two short films (one that was neutral and another that inspired them to feel positive emotions). Then she had them brainstorm a list of all the things they wanted to do right now. Guess who had the longer, more creative lists? The people who had watched the positive film clip. If we extend this theory to a spiritual application, the fruits of the Spirit, feelings like peace and joy, can help us come up with more creative solutions to life's challenges.

Imagine a parent, Sally, who has just come home from a long day of work, gotten dinner together, and now has the challenge of

---

7. D&C 88:118
8. Fredrickson, B. L. (2004). The broaden-and-build theory of positive emotions. *Philosophical Transactions of the Royal Society B: Biological Sciences, 359*(1449), 1367–1377.

providing homework support to her resistant daughter, Greta. Perhaps Sally's a bit worn down, and she burned her hand taking dinner out of the oven. When she checks in on Greta, she sees that she is texting her friends instead of doing math. Sally has warned her about this before, and this time she snaps at her, Greta talks back, and Sally barks, "Get your homework done now or you are grounded!" Consider an alternative scenario—Sally has consciously made an effort to compliment her daughter on putting away her book bag when she got home, thanked her for taking out the dog, and kept a prayer in her heart before approaching the homework situation. She would likely be feeling calmer, and, as a result, she would have more capacity to come up with creative solutions to the problem at hand. She might create a homework charging station, a place for the phone to go during homework, or she might offer to watch a show with Greta if she gets her homework done by 7:30 p.m., or she might grab a book and read at the table so that Greta has some quiet company.

Second, broaden-and-build theory says that positive emotions connect us to other people and help us build social resources. Being connected to other people can literally help us survive over the long haul. People who don't have friends and support from other people are at risk for poor health—in fact, being isolated and lonely without social support has been shown to be more hazardous to our health than smoking![9] Julianne Holt-Lundstad, who researches the effects of loneliness, estimated that social isolation is as hazardous as smoking 15 cigarettes a day.[10] It's not surprising that Christ invites us to "Be one"[11] for both our spiritual health and our physical health. Part of our covenant in following Him is to "bear one another's burdens . . .

---

9. The idea of social support being more hazardous that smoking has been around for a while, as documented by House and colleagues. House, J. S., Landis, K. R., & Umberson, D. (1988). Social relationships and health. *Science, 241*(4865), 540–545. More recently, a meta-analysis by authors from Brigham Young University demonstrated that strong social relationships can increase chances of living longer by 50% compared to those who are isolated. Holt-Lunstad, J., Smith, T. B., & Layton, J. B. (2010). Social relationships and mortality risk: a meta-analytic review. *PLoS medicine, 7*(7), e1000316.

10. CBC News (Aug. 16, 2017). Why loneliness can be as unhealthy as smoking 15 cigarettes a day. http://www.cbc.ca/news/healthloneliness-public-health-psychologist-1.4249637

11. D&C 38:27, see also John 17:21; 4 Nephi 1:17; D&C 35:2

to mourn with those who mourn . . . to comfort those that stand in need of comfort."[12] But notice that these commandments are much easier to follow if we have focused on cultivating positive emotions associated with the Spirit, and conversely, following these commandments will often lead to feeling love, joy, peace, and gratitude. In other words, this is a pattern that can contribute to our happiness, build our capacity, and connect us to community.

The scriptures also say, "The Lord called his people Zion, because they were of one heart and one mind."[13] It's not a coincidence that the Spirit communicates in our mind and in our heart.[14] When we are all feeling the Spirit in our mind and in our hearts—again, the fruit of the Spirit—we feel connected to each other, and we serve each other. When that happens, we experience Zion, which the scripture describes as living in righteousness with no poor among us. In the best-case scenario, a self-reinforcing pattern starts to happen when we feel positive emotions: we connect with other people, we comfort each other and share with each other when someone is in a tight spot, service brings more joy, and the pattern repeats itself.

BIOLOGICAL EFFECTS OF POSITIVE EMOTIONS

So, what happens biologically when we focus on meditating and feeling positive emotions? In our brain, blood floods the prefrontal cortex.[15] The prefrontal cortex is often referred to as the executive center of our brains—this area of the brain focuses on long-term planning, problem-solving, and social connection. Parts of the prefrontal cortex specifically have the job to process emotions. In other words, when the prefrontal cortex is engaged, we can think more creatively and feel more connected with other people. In teens, the prefrontal cortex is

---

12. Mosiah 18:8–9
13. Moses 7:18
14. D&C 8:2
15. Hanson, R. (2009). *Buddha's brain: The practical neuroscience of happiness, love, and wisdom*. Oakland, CA: New Harbinger Publications.

in the process of development, and developing habits to maximize the functioning of this area of the brain could have long-term benefits.[16]

In the last few decades, two areas of research have surged. First, a focus on positive emotions was led by researchers such as Barbara Frederickson and Martin Seligman, who founded the field of positive psychology.[17] Second, brain research has exploded—the '90s were called the decade of the brain, and brain imaging studies have been integrated into many areas of research, including spirituality.[18] While this research is secular in nature, we present some compelling studies through the frame of faith in the gospel that highlight where these two areas of study come together. We also apply these ideas to teaching in family life and practicing patient resilience with teenagers.

COMPASSION

Several studies have found that focusing on loving kindness leads to both emotional and health benefits. In one laboratory, scientists ran an experiment in which they promoted loving kindness through an intervention. Participants met with a trained therapist for one hour a week for six weeks and practiced guided meditation focused on love, compassion, and cultivating goodwill. In addition, they discussed how to apply these principles in daily life and practice meditation on their own. Compared to a group who did not meet, people who practiced the loving kindness meditation were more likely to feel connected to others, and in turn, they had better cardiac health.[19] The authors of this study suggested that this tangible health benefit contributed to "an upward spiral dynamic"—or in other words, consciously focusing

16. Andersen, S. (2016). Commentary on the special issue on the adolescent brain: Adolescence, trajectories, and the importance of prevention. *Neuroscience and Biobehavioral Reviews, 70,* 329–333.

17. Seligman, M. E. (2004). *Authentic happiness: Using the new positive psychology to realize your potential for lasting fulfillment.* New York: Simon and Schuster.

18. Miller, L. (2016). *The spiritual child: The new science on parenting for health and lifelong thriving.* New York: Macmillan.

19. Kok, B. E., Coffey, K. A., Cohn, M. A., Catalino, L. I., Vacharkulksemsuk, T., Algoe, S. B., . . . & Fredrickson, B. L. (2013). How positive emotions build physical health: Perceived positive social connections account for the upward spiral between positive emotions and vagal tone. *Psychological science, 24*(7), 1123–1132.

on loving others, meditating, and practicing led to a self-reinforcing pattern of positive emotions, connection, and health.

When teenagers establish "upward spiral" patterns early in their lives, positive patterns of thinking and feeling can strengthen them during a crucial time of decision-making and across their lives. However, teenagers are surrounded by a pop culture that worships cynicism, sarcasm, and criticism. We are actively teaching them to use those skills to think critically, and their brains have newly developed skill sets that allow them to tear arguments apart. These are important skills, but it is just as important to teach skills of love, compassion, and other positive emotions.

The example of Joseph Smith and Parley P. Pratt is an instructive example of how healing love and understanding can be. In a recent conference talk, Elder Cook described a particularly dark time in Parley P. Pratt's life.[20] He had consecrated all he had, and he lost everything in a national financial crisis that was magnified by local speculation and leaders' financial misjudgments (including Joseph Smith's). Then another devastating loss followed: his young wife, pregnant with their first child, passed away. Struggling under a dark cloud, Parley left, setting off toward Missouri. He met two apostles along the way who convinced him to come back and reconcile with Joseph. Joseph showed him compassion, understanding, and forgiveness—this reunion allowed healing and from the ashes of his despair, Parley built a life of faith and service. This example shines bright as an example of the righteous leadership of both men that spread "gentleness and meekness, and . . . love unfeigned" and an "increase of love" after discord.[21]

For most of us, no one pushes our buttons like family members. The instruction to "the household of faith" to be filled with charity and actively decorate our minds and our lives with virtue is crucial groundwork to be able to support teenagers (and your spouse, parents, brothers and sisters, nieces and nephews).[22] Practicing charity and virtue in everyday situations helps build an upward spiral in families and diffuses the momentum of negative spirals when loved ones go through dark times.

---

20. Cook, Quentin L. (2017). Foundations of Faith. General Conference, April.
21. D&C 121:41–43
22. D&C 121:45

OPTIMISM

President Gordon B. Hinckley counseled, "Cultivate an attitude of happiness. Cultivate a spirit of optimism. Walk with faith, rejoicing in the beauties of nature, in the goodness of those you love, in the testimony which you carry in your heart concerning things divine."[23] Why does optimism matter? Some might argue that looking at life through rose-colored glasses is an illusion. However, this habit of hope and seeing the best in people and in situations has been shown to have powerful benefits. Research evidence has found that optimism is associated with spirituality, or the cultivation of a personal relationship with God. People who nurture optimism tend to cope well with life's stress, experience physical health benefits like healthier immune systems and reduced sensation of pain, and they tend to live longer than pessimists.[24]

The study of optimism began as a reaction to a phenomenon called "learned helplessness." Dr. Martin Seligman had spent several years observing what happened to dogs who had been conditioned to get a mild electric shock after a bell was rung.[25] After a while, the dogs would react to the bell as if they had already been shocked, and when they were put into a divided room with a floor that shocked them, they just laid down without trying to jump the barrier into the safe side of the room. In other words, they just gave up. In contrast, dogs who had not gotten used to being shocked immediately jumped over the barrier to safety. Dogs who had been shocked learned to be helpless and hopeless.

Seligman wondered if helplessness can be learned, can hope and optimism also be learned? He found that in human beings, the way people interpret their failures and negative experiences matters. Three types of interpretations contribute to learned helplessness: the belief that failure is personal, permanent, and global. First, taking a failure personally means believing that the failure happened because of a personal characteristic—for example, I failed that test because I'm stupid

---

23. Hinckley, Gordon B. (1984). "If Thou Art Faithful." General Conference, Oct.

24. Seligman, M. E. (2004). *Authentic happiness: Using the new positive psychology to realize your potential for lasting fulfillment.* New York: Simon and Schuster.

25. Ibid.

(rather than, I failed the test because I didn't study). Second, learned helplessness is associated with seeing failure as a permanent condition rather than temporary—I'll never get a good grade (rather than, this was a tough test, but I'll do better on the next one). Third, when someone is in the mindset of learned helplessness, they tend to see problems as all-encompassing or global—all tests are pointless (rather than, this particular test didn't seem fair). These patterns of thinking put us at risk for spiraling into depression and listlessness.

The good news is that like helplessness, optimism can also be learned. In his book, *Authentic Happiness*, Seligman outlined a process of challenging our negative thinking:

- Be aware of our beliefs, or the story we are telling ourselves. Pay particular attention to thoughts that frame a problem as personal, permanent, and global.
- Be aware of the consequences of negative thought patterns. Thoughts of helplessness feed feelings of anger or fear which can destroy our ability to concentrate and problem-solve, ultimately immobilizing us.
- Argue with yourself. Look for examples that contradict the frame of helpless thinking. In other words, look for evidence that the problem can be changed (it's not personal), it is temporary (not permanent), and it's local (not global).

Let's look at an example. We'll go back to Sally and Greta who has been struggling to do homework. Sally has tried everything she can think of to get Greta to do her homework—Sally has taken away screen time, they have a homework schedule, she has gotten help for her at school, and she keeps a chart of points to help motivate and reward her. In spite of this support, Greta still avoids doing homework. Sally might be tempted to throw her hands in the air at this point and give up. She may be thinking, "Why do I bother? I'm a terrible mother. My kids are never going to get into college." In other words, Sally is starting to fall into the same type of negative spiral we sometimes see in teenagers. She started out with a burnt hand but spiraled into thinking that her kids will never go to college and that it's all her fault. (Notice how mother and daughter's fears may mirror and feed each other.)

Following Seligman's instructions, Sally could first take a deep breath and recognize that she is taking the situation personally when she characterizes herself as a terrible mother. She would also recognize that she feels hopeless when she goes there, which does not help her or her daughter. As she analyzes her thoughts and feelings, she would also recognize that she is defining the problem as permanent and global when she sees the problem as extending years into the future and across all of her children. After becoming aware of these thought patterns, Sally could actively dispute them. She could focus on times that she had parenting wins in this situation—calling to mind the times she has been patient and worked at the kitchen table with Greta while she did her homework. She could recall the visit they had to the museum, or the time Greta shared her enthusiasm for butterflies and they ordered caterpillars to hatch at home. She may also find evidence that this situation is temporary by looking for and identifying all of the classes in the last few years in which Greta has gotten good grades. By specifically noticing the time of day or season that Greta struggles the most, Sally would also be framing the problem as temporary, making it more manageable. All-or-nothing thinking affects both parents and children. Reframing the problem in more optimistic terms would not only help Sally to keep hope front and center and find creative solutions, but it would also model for Greta valuable life lessons about coping with challenge and failure.

In a challenging and cynical world, these lessons of hope and optimism are needed more than ever. In his first address to the BYU student body, President Kevin J. Worthen talked about the importance of successfully failing.[26] He pointed out a part of the BYU mission is "to assist individuals in their quest for perfection and eternal life." But he expressed his concern that "we tend to focus too much on the word perfection and not enough on the word quest." Many teenagers push themselves to succeed and feel a sense of failure because after giving it everything they had, they didn't do well on an AP test or didn't get into the college they wanted. He urged our young people to recognize that when they are in circumstances that they can't control because life

---

26. Worthen, K. J. (5 Jan. 2015). Successfully Failing: Pursuing our Quest for Perfection. Brigham Young University devotional. https://speeches.byu.edu/.

is messy and hard, to remember past accomplishments and their divine heritage. In other words, he reminded us of principles of the gospel that invite us to reframe with optimism. President Worthen concluded by reminding us that the Savior's sacrifice was infinite. He said, "Too often we ask the wrong question when we fail. We ask, 'Am I good enough?' But the real question is 'Is God good enough?' . . . He is. God is as good, as powerful, as loving, as patient, and as consistent as He says He is."

GRATITUDE

Another important emotion to cultivate to protect ourselves and our adolescents is gratitude. Doctrine and Covenants 78:19 reads, "And he who receiveth all things with thankfulness shall be made glorious; and the things of this earth shall be added unto him, even an hundred fold, yea, more." The heart of this scripture is a perspective of gratitude. When we start to focus on all of the blessings we have, we see the things of this earth differently. Maybe creation opens up to us—we savor a beautiful sunset, we're grateful for a stranger's smile, and we notice the new leaves on the trees in springtime. And our relationships change—we reach out to hold hands, we remember to thank our kids for taking out the trash, we recognize our health and strength. Not surprisingly, research has found some positive effects are related to having a perspective of gratitude.

According to those who have researched the effects of gratitude, the blessings of gratitude extend to our mind and our health. A life focused on gratitude has been shown to protect people against depression to some degree. In a review of research about gratitude, the authors of the article state, "A life orientation toward the positive seems incompatible with the 'negative triad' of beliefs about self, world, and future, which is associated with depression."[27] This doesn't mean that a person who is grateful never feels depressed—in fact, Dr. Seligman explains that each person has a different "set point" for happiness, due

---

27. Wood, A. M., Froh, J. J., & Geraghty, A. W. (2010). Gratitude and well-being: A review and theoretical integration. *Clinical psychology review*, *30*(7), 890–905, pg. 4.

to our genetics and the circumstances that we grew up in.[28] However, practicing gratitude may help raise our own personal levels of happiness and reduce the likelihood of developing depression and other psychological disorders. For example, in a large study, religious gratitude was related to lower chances of developing a psychological disorder such as anxiety, an eating disorder, or drug dependence.[29]

Some scientists who study gratitude, think that gratitude might be like a personality trait that cannot really be changed, but others have shown that when we practice gratitude regularly, it changes us. In one study, individuals who had visited a university clinic to get mental health services were assigned to one of three groups: 1) one group wrote letters to other people about what they were grateful for, 2) another group wrote expressively about stressful experiences that they had, 3) and the third group was a control group that did not receive a writing assignment.[30] The group that focused on gratitude had improved mental health four weeks later and twelve weeks later, and their mental health improvements were better than the expressive writing group or the control group. An analysis of the gratitude letters showed that individuals used the word "we" more often, and they tended to use positive language and less negative language compared to the expressive writing. This implies that gratitude connects us to other people and to positive thinking. Even though participants only wrote for twenty minutes once a week for three weeks, this study implies that spending time thinking and writing about gratitude can have a profound change on people weeks later. This doesn't guarantee that we won't get depression or another disorder, and many of us will still need professional help, but it might lower the chances or the severity of a psychological disorder.

---

28. Seligman, M. E. (2004). *Authentic happiness: Using the new positive psychology to realize your potential for lasting fulfillment.* New York: Simon and Schuster.
29. Kendler, K. S., Liu, X. Q., Gardner, C. O., McCullough, M. E., Larson, D., & Prescott, C. A. (2003). Dimensions of religiosity and their relationship to lifetime psychiatric and substance use disorders. *American journal of psychiatry, 160*(3), 496–503.
30. Wong, Y. J., Owen, J., Gabana, N. T., Brown, J. W., Mcinnis, S., Toth, P., & Gilman, L. (2016). Does gratitude writing improve the mental health of psychotherapy clients? Evidence from a randomized controlled trial. *Psychotherapy Research*, 1–11.

In 2007, President Henry B. Eyring gave a talk entitled "O Remember, Remember," and in it, he described an impression he had to write down the blessings for which he was grateful.[31] He described how his perspective changed and he began to look for the hand of the Lord in every day. He said, "More than gratitude began to grow in my heart. Testimony grew. I became ever more certain that our Heavenly Father hears and answers prayers. I felt more gratitude for the softening and refining that come because of the Atonement of the Savior Jesus Christ. And I grew more confident that the Holy Ghost can bring all things to our remembrance—even things we did not notice or pay attention to when they happened." Gratitude leads to other good things. One study found that early adolescents who measured high on gratitude also measured high on forgiveness, optimism, contentment, and inspiration.[32] Gratitude is also related to stronger social connections, which suggests that gratitude could be an effective way to jump start a cascade of positive emotions and connectedness in our lives.

JOY

We create most of our suffering, so it should be logical that we also have the ability to create more joy. It simply depends on the attitudes, the perspectives, and the reactions we bring to situations and to our relationships with other people. When it comes to personal happiness there is a lot that we as individuals can do.
                                            —Dali Lama[33]

The search for joy and happiness cuts across religious beliefs, and the theme of perspective comes up again and again as a path to happiness and resilience. As he closes out his letter to the Philippians, Paul asks these people that he loves dearly to "Rejoice in the Lord alway."[34] Then he gives some advice on how to do that. He says, "Be careful for nothing," or as translated in the New International Version of the bible,

31. Eyring, Henry B. (2007). O, Remember, Remember. General Conference, Oct.
32. Seligman, M. E. (2004). *Authentic happiness: Using the new positive psychology to realize your potential for lasting fulfillment.* New York: Simon and Schuster.
33. 14th Dali Lama, Tutu, D., Abrams, D. (2016). *The Book of Joy.* New York: Avery.
34. Philippians 4:4

"Don't be anxious about anything."[35] Instead, he advises his fellow laborers to do everything in prayer and thanksgiving and to think on things that are lovely, of good report, virtuous, and worthy of praise. If we do this, he promises that the "peace of God, which passes all understanding, shall keep your hearts and minds through Christ Jesus."[36] This "admonition of Paul" is repeated in the 13th Article of Faith, and it reflects the thought, feeling, action cycle that is taught by cognitive behavioral psychologists. Our thoughts lead to our feelings, our feelings lead to our actions, we experience consequences, and as we interpret them, the cycle repeats itself. Interestingly, Paul says a few verses later, "I can do all things through Christ which strengtheneth me."[37] In a cynical world that increasingly focuses on how "cool" it is to be sarcastic and negative, teaching our teenagers to lay aside anxiety by focusing on the positive and gathering strength to act in Christ is needed more than ever before.

In his talk, "Joy and Spiritual Survival," Elder Nelson also echoed Paul when he taught that one type of joy is peace that "passeth all understanding."[38] He emphasized that when we rely on the Savior, we can have joy even in the most difficult times, like the early Saints who found a way to celebrate each other's company even as they were driven out of Missouri. When we step back and look at the big picture, the plan of salvation and the unconditional love and acceptance of our Savior, we find perspective. It's no coincidence that early prophets climbed mountains and found sacred experiences in locations where they could literally see the big picture of the landscape laid out before them. When they stepped away from everyday life and worries, they were able to open their hearts to joy and love, communicate with God, and receive a glimpse of eternity.

As mentioned earlier, each individual has a different personal "set point" or average level of happiness.[39] In other words, some of us have

---

35. Philippians 4:6
36. Philippians 4:7
37. Philippians 4:13
38. Nelson, R. M. (2016). Joy and Spiritual Survival. General Conference, Oct.
39. Lyubomirsky, S., Sheldon, K. M., & Schkade, D. (2005). Pursuing happiness: The architecture of sustainable change. *Review of general psychology, 9*(2), 111–131. Seligman, M. E. (2004). *Authentic happiness: Using the new positive psychology to realize your potential for lasting fulfillment.* New York: Simon and Schuster.

a personality that is a bit sunnier or a bit cloudier on average. Studies with identical and fraternal twins have shown us that genetics determines about 50% of the variation in happiness.[39] Our circumstances contribute only about 10% of the variance in happiness —we might get bit of a bump if we get a raise or a bit of a slump if we experience health challenges, but most of us settle back to our set point after a while. What we do —our actions —determine the remaining 40% of variance in happiness. What can we do to increase happiness? Personal exercise makes a difference; so do our patterns of thinking. A relatively new area of study focuses on developing values of gratitude and optimism. Those who participated in 6-week interventions of regularly writing letters of gratitude or writing optimistically about the future demonstrated an increased sense of being in control of life and being connected to other people compared to those who wrote about the past. As a result, people who participated reported a sense of life satisfaction—what we might call joy.[40] In other words, as the gospel teaches us, each of us can consciously create habits in our lives that raise our personal feelings of peace, optimism, contentment, and joy, regardless of our circumstances. This does not mean that our problems disappear, our relationships are "fixed," or mental health issues, including depression, magically diappear. Rather, for some, it can increase joy a bit, giving us hope for the future.

Much of the rest of this book focuses on habits or practices that can help us (and our teenagers) to maximize the joy in our lives. In Part 2, we focus specifically on parenting practices. We start with practical parenting tips (Chapter 4), then we continue with the idea of practicing balance (Chapter 5), and then turn to promoting spirituality in our youth (Chapter 6).

---

40. Boehm, J. K., Lyubomirsky, S., & Sheldon, K. M. (2011). A longitudinal experimental study comparing the effectiveness of happiness-enhancing strategies in Anglo Americans and Asian Americans. *Cognition & Emotion, 25*(7), 1263–1272.

PART ❷

Parenting Practices

CHAPTER 4

Parenting Teenagers

Have you ever noticed that there is a wealth of information out there on parenting babies and preschoolers, but very little guidance on how to parent teenagers? Yet, today, parents often get blamed for their teenager's problems or mistakes. When parents feel like no matter what they do, it is never enough, they are in danger of parental burnout. For parents who are feeling burnt out, the thinking goes like this: If nothing you do works, why do anything at all? In the high-pressure world of parenting, parental burnout has been identified as a phenomenon characterized by exhaustion, emotional distancing, and a sense of parenting ineffectiveness.[1] When parenting seems overwhelming, breaking down parenting into a set of skills and practices that we can focus on one at a time may help. In this chapter, we concentrate on timeless principles of parenting, with emphasis on the behaviors and attitudes that will help us run the marathon with patience. In this paragraph, we outline some of the evidence-based parenting techniques that have been shown to work best with teenagers. Our goal is not to encourage a high-pressure parenting style or suggest that you have been doing it wrong all along, but rather to

---

1. Roskam, I., Raes, M. E., & Mikolajczak, M. (2017). Exhausted parents: development and preliminary validation of the parental burnout inventory. *Frontiers in psychology, 8,* article 163.

provide tools that you can pick up one at a time and apply to common challenges you face with your teens. In the next pages, we focus on being positive with our youth, strengthening communication, being strategic about discipline, and understanding adolescent challenges.

POSITIVE PARENTING

The foundation for positive parenting is a warm, supportive relationship. Without warmth and trust in parent-child relationships, guidance and discipline may not work effectively. Because our brains tend to focus on the negative, as parents we have to actively fight the habit of honing in on all of the things our kids aren't doing or the things that need correcting. Think of how excited and encouraging we were when our kids were learning to walk. Every effort inspired smiles and cheers, right? Teenagers need that same positive support.

Studies have shown that focusing on at least three positive interactions to every negative interaction is important for creating a warm, creative environment.[2] An evidence-based parenting program recommends aiming for a 4:1 ratio of positives to negatives.[3] This might mean that you catch your teenager doing something good, like emptying the dishwasher, staying calm when Dad was late to pick them up, or getting good grades. A simple thank you, a quick squeeze, or some quality time with parents can be rewarding to teenagers. Some parents might argue that we shouldn't give compliments for living up to basic expectations. However, if we focus only on the things that need to improve, then teens often feel nagged or nitpicked, which can create resentment and a resistance to engage in basic expectations. If parents then follow up with harsh punishment, it can create a power struggle, and things can spiral down from there. In evidence-based parenting interventions, parents are encouraged to focus on the positive things

---

2. Fredrickson, B. L. (2004). The broaden-and-build theory of positive emotions. *Philosophical Transactions of the Royal Society B: Biological Sciences, 359* (1449), 1367–1377.
3. Dishion, T. J., Stormshak, E. A., & Kavanagh, K. A. (2012). *Everyday parenting: A professional's guide to building family management skills*. Research Press.

their children are doing before working on discipline issues—a strong, positive relationship is critical to successful parenting.[4]

When Jen attended BYU, one of the family science professors shared a practical way to remember how many positive things you said to a child compared to negative comments. He suggested keeping nine neutral colored rubber bands on your wrist, and one red one. Every time you compliment your child, thank them or give them praise, move a neutral band over to your other wrist. Ideally, all nine neutral rubber bands are on the opposite wrist before you critique your teen or say something negative. In this way, we are intentionally filling our loved ones' emotional buckets, which creates a positive atmosphere in our homes and helps us practice charity. Another suggested practice is pennies in one pocket switched to another pocket.

Not surprisingly, the scriptures give us guidance for positive parenting: The last ten verses of Doctrine and Covenants 121 can be considered a treatise on parenting.[5] Both parents have access to priesthood power and have authority in the home,[6] and these verses instruct us on how to connect with the powers of heaven in our parenting: "The rights of the priesthood are inseparably connected with the powers of heaven, and the powers of heaven cannot be controlled nor handled only upon the principles of righteousness."[7] The qualities we are specifically instructed to cultivate are "persuasion, . . . long-suffering, . . . gentleness, . . . meekness, and . . . love unfeigned."[8] We are advised to avoid "control or dominion or compulsion" because the Spirit withdraws.[9] In other words, when we use coercion, forcing our kids to do things or controlling them, we are not maximizing the opportunity to receive inspiration. That is not to say that discipline should be ignored—it is definitely important, but discipline works better in the framework of a positive atmosphere with good communication. Furthermore, we

---

4. Patterson, G. R., Forgatch, M. S., & DeGarmo, D. S. (2010). Cascading effects following intervention. *Development and psychopathology, 22*(4), 949–970.
5. D&C 121:34–46
6. Oaks, D. H. (2020). The Melchizedek Priesthood and the Keys. General Conference, Apr. See also, Oaks, D. H. (2014). The keys and authority of the priesthood. General Conference, Apr.
7. D&C 121:36
8. D&C 121:41
9. D&C 121: 37

know from research that control might work in the short term, but it backfires as a parenting strategy in the long term.[10]

While small, consistent rewards can be really useful to help a teen establish a new habit, we'd like to share a word of caution when it comes to rewards. Holding out carrots or giving big rewards for kids to do things can actually decrease a teen's internal motivation to do something.[11] We want to support recognition of the internal satisfaction of a job well done whenever possible. This is especially important in spiritual things—we are hoping the teen recognizes the peace and fruit of the Spirit rather than expecting an outside reward. For example, if a parent promises a young person a brand-new car upon completing four years of seminary, that could actually send the message that attending seminary is not worth it on its own. On the other hand, Helaman reminds us that "by small and simple things, great things are brought to pass."[12] A small reward after a successful week of attending seminary is likely to be helpful, especially when establishing a new habit. A parent might say, "I'm really proud of you for getting up on your own this week" or "Let's make an ice-cream run to celebrate going to seminary every day this week."

Another proven parenting strategy is spending positive time together each week, which falls under "wholesome recreational activities" recommended in the Proclamation to the Family.[13] This could be a formal, planned parent-child "date." Parent-child dates work best when the parent lets the teenager lead in choosing an activity that they enjoy doing. It doesn't have to be expensive or take a lot of time, but brainstorming what interests the teen is important. This might mean

---

10. Patterson, G. R. (2016). Coercion theory. In T. J. Dishion & J. Snyder (Eds.), *The Oxford Handbook of Coercive Relationship Dynamics* (Vol. *1*). New York, NY: Oxford University Press. doi:10.1093/oxfordhb/9780199324552.013.2. See also, Mehus, C. J., Doty, J., Chan, G., Kelly, A. B., Hemphill, S., Toumbourou, J., & McMorris, B. J. (2018). Testing the social interaction learning model's applicability to adolescent substance misuse in an Australian context. *Substance use & misuse, 53*(11), 1859–1868.

11. Ryan, R. M., & Deci, E. L. (2000). Self-determination theory and the facilitation of intrinsic motivation, social development, and well-being. *American psychologist, 55*(1), 68–78.

12. Alma 37:6

13. The First Presidency of the Church of Jesus Christ of Latter-day Saints. (1995). The family: A proclamation to the world.

that a dad watches old reruns of SpongeBob with his daughter instead of that new documentary that would be educational for her. Or maybe a mom teaches her son to drive a stick shift in an empty parking lot instead of taking him to an art museum. If a documentary or art museum is what the teen wants to do, great! Relationship experts have found that if a relationship is rocky, working on problems doesn't necessarily improve the relationship. However, when people actively build experiences they enjoy into their relationships, they are more likely to thrive.[14] In other words, having fun together is important!

Jen's family has named this type of parent-child outing a "coaching session" as a reminder that parents can learn from good coaches that work with young people. The best coaches look for strengths and maximize those strengths on the field, but they also look for opportunities to correct and motivate to help players improve their skills. Jen says, "One of our daughter's coaches led a winning soccer team for a number of years, and every player who walked on that team got a chance to play in a spot that maximized their talents. The coach was positive, but he also corrected and demonstrated techniques to help each player improve. Above all, he taught the girls to play together as a team—for example in scrimmages, he gave two points to a goal that was scored on a pass. In games, practice paid off, and the team worked together with each player contributing their best to win. As parents, we try to take the mindset of a coach as we spend time with them, focus on recognizing and developing our children's strengths and teaching them to be team players, while occasionally showing them how a correction will help them improve their performance.

COMMUNICATION

Communication is a critical aspect of good relationships with teenagers. Most research that asks about close parent-child relationships in the teen years also asks questions like, "Can you talk to your mom or dad about your problems?" or rate the statement, "I can count on

---

14. Building on John Gottman's research: Lisitsa, Ellie. (7 Nov. 2012). The Sound Relationship House: Build Love Maps. *The Gottman Institute.* https://www.gottman.com/blog/the-sound-relationship-house-build-love-maps/.

my mom/dad when I need to get something off my chest." In 2009, Elder Ballard gave a talk entitled, "Fathers and Sons: A Remarkable Relationship."[15] Here is some of his advice about communicating:

Fathers, listen to your sons—really listen to them. Ask the right kind of questions, and listen to what your sons have to say each time you have a few minutes together. You need to know—not to guess but to know—what is going on in your son's life. Don't assume that you know how he feels just because you were young once. Your sons live in a very different world from the one in which you grew up. As they share with you what's going on, you will have to listen very carefully and without being judgmental in order to understand what they are thinking and experiencing.

He reminds fathers to fight the urge to fix problems when a son shares them but to just listen. In fact, he repeats the advice to listen at least four times in that talk, and he says, "Remember, conversation where you do 90 percent of the talking is not a conversation."[101] This is great advice that applies to mothers and daughters as well.

A great resource for improving communication about important, but emotionally challenging issues is the book *Crucial Conversations: Tools for Talking When the Stakes are High.*[16] The authors outline seven steps for approaching tough conversations successfully. The beauty of their method is that instead of just emphasizing the importance of communication, they actually break down the skills needed to communicate in the most difficult of circumstances. Here is a brief overview of their recommendations:

1. Start with heart—Make a commitment to stick with what you want to get out of the conversation for yourself, your teen, and your relationship. The authors encourage you to ask yourself, "How would I behave if I really wanted these results?"

2. Learn to look—Be on the lookout for signs that the conversation is not safe. This usually means at least one member of the

---

15. Ballard, M. J. (2009). Fathers and sons: A remarkable relationship. General Conference, Oct.

16. Patterson, K. (2002). *Crucial conversations: Tools for talking when stakes are high.* Tata McGraw-Hill Education.

family is retreating or attacking—you might recognize physical signs of stress in yourself: your heart rate has gone up, your palms are sweating.

3. Make it safe—Acknowledge the need for safety and a mutual purpose for having the conversation. This may mean recognizing failures to respect the other's point of view or feelings, and apologizing.

4. Master your story—Be aware of the stories we tell ourselves that fuel our emotions. Analyzing our stories to see how they fuel our emotions and the "facts" that we are reacting to allows us to reach our mutual goals for the conversation.

5. State your path—Speak honestly with humility and share the facts as you see them, checking in to get the other person's perspective. Recognize that your story is not necessarily reality.

6. Explore others' paths—When your adolescent reacts by blowing up or shutting down, express interest in their side of the story. Respectfully validate their feelings; in other words, mirror back to them what you think they are feeling. Paraphrase by summing up what they have said. If these steps still don't work, try to tentatively guess what they might be feeling.

7. Move to action—Decisions need to be made daily in families, and most of them don't need everyone's input, but it's important to identify when to get adolescents' opinions, when to give them a voice in decision-making, and when to spend the time coming to consensus as a family. Checking in to see if they care will give you that information.

Although these steps were originally developed for business settings, thinking carefully about the process of our communication is equally helpful in family settings. Having regular one-on-one time with teens and family councils provides an open space to explore some issues and decisions.

Here, we go in depth on a couple of the skills that often can be a barrier when a parent-teen relationship is tense. The first is "master your stories." The authors of *Crucial Conversations* say, "While it's true that at first we are in control of the stories we tell—after all, we do make them up of our own accord—once they're told, the stories control us" (p. 101).[16] Jessica was talking with a friend who joked that he hoped his child enjoyed checking out a cop car during a field trip because he was so "bad" that he'd probably be "riding in it someday." What's scary is that a parent's viewpoint is powerful enough to contribute to that outcome. If the stories you have in your head about your child's future are consistently negative, it's important that you start trying to find a new narrative. It might be helpful to find a good therapist who can help you reframe your stories. Checking our thoughts and assumptions about our teens can be part of the process of approaching them "full of charity" with "love unfeigned" as recommended in Doctrine and Covenants 121.[17] Choosing to challenge our negative stories about our kids will help us to avoid a boiling anger that bubbles over into sarcasm or outright yelling at our teens. It will also help us to avoid jumping to negative conclusions.

This is so important! Once Jen found a hidden search software one of her kids was using on the computer. Her imagination went wild—the stories she was telling herself were scary. She took some time to check in with her husband, Matthew, and talk through their strategy. They prayerfully decided to take a curious approach rather than a confrontational approach. When she and Matthew sat down to talk with their teen, the kid explained they were concerned about government scanning their searches. Microsoft Family, a monitoring software, had a record of their searches, and they were able to go through the search history together with their child and verify that they hadn't gotten into dangerous places online. If as parents they had assumed the worst, trust in the relationship would have eroded badly. Notice, though, that they still had a way to verify the online history.

Each child is different. Some of our children wear their heart on their sleeve, while others carefully guard their feelings. What about silent, stoic types? Boys in particular are trained not to share emotions in our society. One researcher, Niobe Way, interviewed hundreds of teenage boys, and the boys described becoming increasingly isolated the older they got. They wanted a best friend to share things with, but

---

17. D&C 121:41, 45

they didn't feel like they could. One boy stated, "It might be nice to be a girl because then you wouldn't have to be emotionless."[18] In the book *Raising Cain: Protecting the Emotional Life of Boys*, Dan Kindlon suggests using statements to elicit responses.[19] This is also the sixth *Crucial Conversations* step, "Explore other's feelings."[16] Using tentative language with this tactic is very important; for example, *"I'm not sure if I've got this right, but my best guess is that* you are feeling like we are just trying to control your life." Often if a parent guesses right, the child will explain why that is the case. When a child has shut down, and nothing else works to get them talking, we sometimes use multiple choice questions or true false statements. Depending on the situation, it can help to work a little humor into those multiple choice questions by throwing in some exaggeration. For example, one option might be, "You feel that I ignored your idea like a double-wide Mac truck barreling down the highway going 98 miles an hour." A tentative approach will also likely be helpful. Brené Brown frames these conversations with the phrase, "The story I'm telling myself right now . . ."[20] This approach acknowledges that your thoughts may be totally wrong, but it gets the dialog started.

Another critical skill is apologizing early and often. Sometimes when we are hurt, we nurture our feelings of hurt by keeping the other person's offenses in the forefront of our mind and stoking that fire. Nurturing our stories of others' offenses allows us to avoid any feelings of shame or guilt about our contribution to the situation. This pattern of pride can become an emotional game of chicken, where each person risks damaging the relationship, with the stakes becoming higher the longer it takes to apologize and make up. Ether 12:27 teaches us that if we are daily trying to turn to Christ, He will help

---

18. Way, N. (2013). The hearts of boys. *Contexts*, *12*(1), 14–23. See also the following videos on Youtube: The Crisis of Connection for Adolescent Boys (3 Oct. 2013), https://www.youtube.com/watch?v=7ScAvJ0KiyU, and a TedMed talk: Why "boys will be boys" is a myth—and a harmful one at that (13 Jun. 2019), https://www. youtube.com/watch?v=ydzfQ1X7ips.

19. Kindlon, D. J., & Thompson, M. (2000). *Raising Cain: Protecting the emotional life of boys*. Random House Digital, Inc.

20. Brown, B. (2015). *Rising strong*. Random House. See also a YouTube clip from Soul Sunday: The Stories We Tell Ourselves (25 Nov. 2015), https://www.youtube.com/ watch?v=WyK537UA_E8.

us to humble ourselves, and make our weaknesses our strengths. One practical way we can do that is to ask for help with seeing what we could have done better in any given situation. Other times, we know all too well what we have done to offend, like when we've obviously lost our temper with our kids or spouse. The sooner we acknowledge our mistake and apologize, the better. When parents model this pattern in family life, teenagers learn that apologies are not a way of losing face, but an everyday way of repairing our relationships when we make mistakes. In fact, whenever we communicate with our kids, as parents we are modeling relationship skills to our teens.

STRATEGIC DISCIPLINE

Strategic discipline starts with communicating expectations and consequences clearly. In line with the best parenting practices, this involves getting input from children, and especially teens who are beginning to develop independence. Then, consistency and following through with consequences provides stability and a sense of security for adolescents, even as they sometimes push against the rules. This next section of the chapter handles setting up expectations, discipline, and consequences.

Setting up expectations early helps us as parents to not react in the moment when we are angry with an unreasonable consequence. Whether formal or informal, a family council to set up new house rules or reassess current house rules can be helpful. This gives teens a safe time/place to share their opinions and ideas about current rules, and we know that children who feel like their voice is listened to in family matters tend to have better outcomes.[21] Family councils also give parents a chance to explain why the rule or standard is important—when kids understand that parents are motivated out of love and have their long-term interests at heart, they are more likely to get on board. Here are a few guidelines that we have found helpful:

---

21. Duncan, L. G., Coatsworth, J. D., & Greenberg, M. T. (2009). A model of mindful parenting: Implications for parent–child relationships and prevention research. *Clinical child and family psychology review, 12*(3), 255–270.

1. If possible, have the consequence match the offense. For example, if you don't bring the car home when you promised to, you can't drive it next weekend.

2. Keep consequences small and simple. For example, taking away a cell phone for 24 hours may be just as effective as taking a cell phone away for two weeks, and it will be more realistic to enforce, especially if you have to communicate about rides later in the week.

3. Be open to negotiation, especially on non-essential rules. Maybe going to ward activities is not required but going to sacrament meeting is required.

4. Avoid ultimatums. For example, the following statement is an ultimatum: "If you get tattoos, you will have to move out of the house." If a teen tests the parents' resolve to go through with the ultimatum, it puts parents in the awful situation of either kicking their child out if they get a tattoo or losing credibility.

5. Consider linking privileges to responsibility, especially as adolescents get older. For example, you take on more chores when you turn 12, but you also get to stay up later.

Once you have negotiated some basic family rules, recording and posting them in a place where everyone can refer to them later will reinforce clarity and consistency.

On a day-to-day basis, one important communication skill that is often overlooked is how to make a request for our kids to do something they need to do. Often, we find ourselves yelling across the house, "Time to do your homework!" or "You need to clean the bathroom before getting on screens." The simple fact is that it's really easy to ignore a distant voice in the background, including texts. How you approach your child makes a huge difference. In *Everyday Parenting*, a book of evidence-based strategies for parents,[22] the following is recommended:

---

22. Dishion, T. J., Stormshak, E. A., & Kavanagh, K. A. (2012). *Everyday parenting: A professional's guide to building family management skills*. Research Press.

1. First, go to where your teen is and make sure you have eye contact. You might need to tap them on the shoulder or ask for their attention if they are in the middle of something. For example, you might say, "Do you have a sec?"

2. When they look up, make the request. The request should be simple and direct, not a question. For example, you might state, "It's five o'clock, and we agreed that you would start working on homework before dinner. Please turn off the TV and get started now."

3. Avoid questions which your child could see as optional such as, "Can you get started now?"

4. Monitor to make sure they follow through.

5. Thank them for following through.

Asking the right way will solve many of the problems we have of kids not listening and doing what we ask.

But what happens when we ask, and they still don't follow through? At this point, you could calmly restate the request with a warning that a consequence will follow if they don't comply. For example, Doug is getting ready for dinner, and his daughter Jean is responsible for emptying the dishwasher so that the family can load dishes after dinner. Doug walks over to where Jean is sitting on the coach watching YouTube on her phone. He taps her on the shoulder and makes the request, "Please unload the dishwasher now." Still staring at her phone, Jean holds up her hand and says, "Wait a minute." Her dad replies, "It really needs to be done now, before dinner. Please take a break and unload now." When Jean does not reply, Doug says, "If you don't get it done now, you will lose your phone for 24 hours." (Another strategy is to refer to your clearly defined list of expectations for screen time or a contract of house rules that you wrote down in your most recent family council.) Jean gets up, complaining loudly, but she unloads the dishwasher. At this point maybe Doug is sick of the attitude, but if he lays into her, next time Jean will not want to comply next time. We suggest ignoring the complaining and simply thanking her for getting the chore done—the main goal here is to reinforce the positive behavior. Then the next time she gets the chore done without complaining, Doug might say, "Thanks for getting that done with a good attitude."

Reinforcing positive expressions of empathy and prosocial behavior and ignoring some of the negative emotions/behavior helps us to see our teens in a positive light. The goal is ultimately to be able to see them the way Christ sees them, with divine potential. When we are faced with daily battles month after month, year after year, it's easy to get worn down. What keeps us from mentally defining a teen as a narcissistic, awful human with no future? At times, this may take active efforts on our part to remind ourselves of the positive qualities our kids have. Focusing a nightly gratitude journal on your child or actively remembering your best memories of them may help.

When our kids need correcting, in Doctrine and Covenants 121 the word "betimes" is used. The dictionary lists one meaning for this archaic word as "early." This meaning would imply that the earlier we intervene in a problem situation, the easier it is to correct. Elder Uchtdorf made this point in his talk "A Matter of a Few Degrees," when he said, "The longer we delay corrective action, the larger the needed changes become, and the longer it takes to get back on the correct course."[23] The other meaning of the word "betimes" is "on occasion," which also applies—as parents, we need to pick our battles. If we want to have at least a three to one ratio of positive to negative comments, we'll have to let some minor things go. We might try to shape behavior by catching our teens being good rather than pointing out what they have done wrong.

When our teenagers break the rules, the next part of the scripture in Doctrine and Covenants 121 is also important: "when moved upon by the Holy Ghost."[24] If you are feeling the Spirit while "reproving," you are feeling hopeful, motivated, and loving. If you feel angry or out of control, it will be difficult to feel the Spirit and difficult for your child to feel loved. Jessica notices, "The times I feel the Spirit and the most motivated to change, I feel hopeful, courageous to try to do things differently, and ultimately I am more successful. When I feel I am not good enough or can't change, I typically don't." How do

---

23. Uchtdorf, D. F. (2008). A matter of a few degrees. General Conference, Apr.
24. D&C 121:43

we get in that mindset when we are so tired of battling our kids? One way is to prepare for difficult conversations. Talk to a trusted friend or bishop and outline your concerns, but don't just look for an ally who jumps on board with your frustration. Talk about your love for the child, pray for your child, and imagine them as a future adult who seeks a relationship with you.

That leads to the next part of the scripture: "Then showing forth afterwards an increase of love toward him whom thou hast reproved, lest he esteem thee to be his enemy."[111] This phrase in the scripture captures an amazing parenting principle. When you are in a constant parenting battle, it is easy to feel that your relationship is all about that struggle. If you find yourself constantly circling around the same negative thoughts about your child, look for ways to replace the thoughts. A cognitive principle in therapy is to look for exceptions to any "always and never" thinking. In other words, look for times when your child did what they were supposed to—what was it about that situation that supported their positive behavior? Another principle in cognitive theory is to watch for tunnel vision. When your child is consistently on screens, doesn't do something you want them to do, or is verbally aggressive, it can be easy to focus on your frustration even after we give a healthy consequence. Doing so makes showing an increase of love difficult. Instead focus on her strengths, make time to be one on one together and not talk about the problem, look for ways to build her self-concept, and think about her potential as a child of God.

PRACTICING ENDURANCE IN PARENTING TEENS

When it comes to adolescents, sometimes it's easier for leaders, teachers, and professionals to be optimistic than it is for parents to be optimistic. We have all heard the statement that "No other success can compensate for failure in the home."[25] When parents encounter the failures that inevitably come when we are trying to be celestial parents

---

25. McKay, David O., quoting James Edward McCulloch, in Conference Report, Apr. 1935, 166.

in a telestial world,[26] it can be easy to have a negative spiral that brings us into helpless thought patterns. Elder Rasband reframed this classic statement by redefining success for parents. In a stake conference shortly after he became an apostle, he told parents that as long as they never give up, they are not failing as parents.[27] Reading this book demonstrates your desire to parent better and connect with your child. If we are never going to give up, we need to patiently practice and cultivate optimism in our relationships. One way we can cultivate optimism is by being gentle with parents around us. When we are gentle with others and resist the urge to criticize in our heads, out loud or to others about others' parenting, it helps everyone. We are gentler with ourselves when we talk to and about others in a kind way. When we are looking at others' flaws, our own are more apparent. If we are looking at someone's snapshot moment and judge something so sensitive as parenting, we will hurt not only our ability to connect with them but also our own spirit.

For those of us who struggle with an all-or-nothing attitude, we advocate trying on a "Mom Enough" attitude. This might mean that there are days when the kids are clothed and fed, and that is good enough. We love the parenting website run by a mother-daughter pair who advocate this approach called *MomEnough*.[28] Marti Erickson founded the Children, Youth and Family Consortium at the University of Minnesota, and Erin Erickson is a health practitioner. Their site encourages mothers to take care of themselves and to be patient with themselves. In addition, they provide a wealth of information on their website for parents of both younger children and teens. We appreciate this because the message is to accept where you are at, but to also invest in your parenting. Relying on the Savior helps us learn step by step how to face challenges as they come up.

---

26. Maxwell, Neal A. (1976). Not Withstanding My Weakness. General Conference, Oct.
27. Rasband, R. A. (May, 2016). Lakeville Minnesota Stake Conference.
28. http://momenough.com/

CHAPTER ⑤

Finding Balance in Our Parenting

As parents and professionals who work to promote youth health, we love that the new youth program is focused on helping youth to "grow in a balanced way." Jen had a bishop while she was a student at BYU who was blind. Even so, he had been a psychologist and could see the need for students to find balance in their lives. He encouraged them to make goals in balanced areas of their lives—and it was a blessing. She looks back now and sees benefits of making goals in the 5 areas he suggested focusing on: physical, emotional, academic, social, and spiritual. Similarly, the new youth program encourages us to support balance in the lives of our youth—one of the best ways to do that is to practice balance in our own lives.

In 2 Nephi 2:11 it states:

For it must needs be, that there is an opposition in all things. If not so . . . righteousness could not be brought to pass, neither wickedness, neither holiness nor misery, neither good nor bad. Wherefore, all things must needs be a compound in one; wherefore, if it should be one body it must needs remain as dead, having no life neither death, nor corruption nor incorruption, happiness nor misery, neither sense nor insensibility.

Let's contemplate the context. Lehi was dying; he was speaking to his son who had endured the harsh reality of fleeing in the wilderness, crossing the ocean and extreme conflict in his family. How does the principle of opposition apply to parenting adolescents? In the next sections, we explore the idea of finding balance as we parent and face challenges.

PRINCIPLES OF PUSH AND PULL IN PARENTING

Parenting is a lot like yoga in some ways. In our yoga class, the teacher taught that as we strengthen ourselves, we need to both push and release. This concept has stuck with us as universal. In most yoga poses, you both try to maintain a sense of balance and strength while simultaneously releasing tension. As we practice the push-pull of yoga, we can slide into meditation easier. From Jessica's perspective, "I have found that during yoga, if I have been focused on pushing myself and trying to do certain postures, it is more difficult to calm my brain and meditate. Simultaneously, if I have not pushed myself at all, my body is not ready to meditate when I come to that part of my practice." In parenting, we push our kids and want them to do their best, but we also have to be willing to release them to make their own choices. In working with parents over the years as a therapist, Jessica has noticed that some of us are better pushers and some better releasers. None of us are perfect and neither one is really better than another. The balance of both is what children need as they develop.

PUSH

Why do we push our teenagers? We see their potential. We have hoped for their future since before they were born. Also, societal pressure tells us that our children's success is a measure of our parenting (and conversely that our children's mistakes are a reflection of our parenting).[1] We make a difference in our children's lives in the way we parent and interact with our children. Pushing them to develop feelings of respect and boundaries creates lifetime patterns that will serve them well. Pushing them to be kind and sensitive to the emotions of others will help them with their roommates, families, and work environment. Pushing children to learn the value of money, hard work, and service also teaches life lessons. Some ways parents can help children develop emotions of respect and kindness are engaging the family in serving meals at shelters, helping out at a hospital or places where people are vulnerable, helping refugees, or seeing ministering assignments as a family assignment to feel love and compassion for others. The app Justserve shows opportunities as small as gathering books for those in need and as long-term as befriending vulnerable people. Parents' support can promote "prosocial" experiences that benefit our kids in the long run.[2]

As parents, we often seek out experiences that will allow our kids to learn and grow. However, there is a distinction between making a difference in our children's lives and an outcome of how a child "turns out." Jessica shares, "As I have counseled with patients who feel extreme guilt for children's actions, I have often said that if you do not take responsibility for every positive action your child makes, you cannot take responsibility for every negative one." Have you ever heard a parent exclaim, "My child [insert caught the ball at the football game, aced a test, said something nice, graduated, got a job] because I am a good parent?" Probably not. But I have heard parents ask the question, "What do you think I did that caused my child to suffer from [anxiety, depression, drug addiction]?" Considering the biology, societal influences, and life circumstances that go into personality development and mental health, one factor, such as parenting, could never be isolated as being the cause for children's problems.

1. Coleman, J. (2015). Parenting adult children in the twenty-first century. In B. J. Risman & V. E. Rutter (Eds.) *Families as they really are*, 2nd Ed., New York: W. W. Norton & Company, 390–401.
2. Padilla-Walker, L. M., & Christensen, K. J. (2011). Empathy and self-regulation as mediators between parenting and adolescents' prosocial behavior toward strangers, friends, and family. *Journal of Research on Adolescence*, 21(3), 545–551.

Additionally, Jessica often tells parents she is counseling that children would be destroyed by perfect parents. If a parent was perfect (no mistakes . . . ever), a child would not be able to accept their own imperfections. A parent who can talk about and accept their own limitations by apologizing for mistakes and showing growth with setbacks will assist a child in accepting their own humanity and fallibility. The only perfect parent is our Father in Heaven who sent His Son to live through the mistakes of others and the harshness of the world. Sometimes, the need to create perfect parenting comes from societal pressure to "do it right," and sometimes it comes from having a difficult childhood and wanting your children to have a better start than you did. Whatever the reason you are hard on yourself about parenting—be gentle. Trying hard, learning out of the best books, asking for help when you need it, and looking to good examples around you are all excellent ideas. But if you are creating an environment of self-hate because of your shortcomings, it will not help your child.

So, what can you do if that is the spot you find yourself in? Get help, surround yourself with parents who "get it," who give you slack, and show you love. In one study, when mothers were asked to problem-solve in a lab setting, they did better when they had a confidant in the room.[3] Jessica learned the importance of getting help when her oldest was born: "After 4 years of hoping for him, I thought that I would fall in love with him and love parenting instantly. Instead, I was a nervous wreck. About 5 months into the parenting gig, I met a wonderful friend who was a 'natural.' She and I would hang out. Parenting our toddlers side by side taught me more than most parenting books. Now, that baby is headed to college, and I find myself searching for and spending time with women who 'get it' and are parenting our young adults side by side." She has also noticed that the "tribe" for parenting teens and young adults is more reticent to talk about struggles: their own and their teens.' Some of the reticence is healthy. Creating privacy for teens and young adults is necessary for healthy development. While one can talk about failure to put a

---

3. Forgatch, M. S., & DeGarmo, D. S. (1997). Adult problem solving: Contributor to parenting and child outcomes in divorced families. *Social Development*, *6*(2), 238–254.

child down for a nap and a subsequent meltdown, it is not wise to talk about a teens' meltdown in the same terms, and a teen meltdown can be much more intimidating to a parent. And yet, finding a tribe of people who support you and your child is essential. Sometimes that is the people at church, sometimes it is family members, sometimes it is a neighborhood, book club, school group, or sometimes it is a formal parenting or support group. Sometimes our good friends give us the push we need as parents or the permission to release.

MOTIVATING RATHER THAN PUSHING

While a gentle or even a firm push in the right direction might be helpful for our teen sometimes, more often than not other strategies of motivation work best as our kids get older. As children enter late adolescence and early adulthood, parents' need to guide versus control is essential. Winning a power struggle is usually not worth it if the relationship suffers. Children are creating their future adult relationship with you as you attempt both to be a source of lifelong guidance and comfort. When parents practice principles of motivation, we encourage engagement without pushing our teenagers. We can encourage self-motivation by helping them discover their interests, cultivating a culture of effort, and nurturing a vision of their possible selves.

Have you ever noticed that many teens have an area of interest that sparks excitement in them? For instance, your daughter might light up when she talks about astronomy, and while she might have a tendency to neglect chores or history assignments, she will spend hours on her star finder app or building a telescope. Maybe your son spends hours researching horror makeup and then more hours practicing on himself and all of his friends. Teens who have identified "sparks" tend to benefit—they are more motivated at school, have more friends, and report being more optimistic about the future than those who don't have "sparks."[4] In the Doctrine and Covenants, this type of passion to understand, learn, and create is described as light—a God-given gift: "And the light which shineth, which giveth you light, is through him

---

4. Scales, P. C., Benson, P. L., & Roehlkepartain, E. C. (2011). Adolescent thriving: The role of sparks, relationships, and empowerment. *Journal of Youth and Adolescence, 40*(3), 263–277.

who enlighteneth your eyes, which is the same light that quickeneth your understandings."[5] Learning happens faster, "quicker," when we are motivated.

As parents, one thing we can do for our youth is encourage the development of this type of spark and help them connect it to the efforts they make at home, at school, and at church. For example, one young woman we know loves scary movies—her parents supported her idea to turn their backyard into a haunted walk on Halloween. She turned this project into a Personal Progress project,[6] which although unconventional, helped her learn skills in organizing events and served the families in the neighborhood.

When it comes to hard work, having an enduring spark of interest can help motivation but let's face it, learning—whether spiritual, social, or academic—sometimes requires struggle and effort. Another way we can support motivation is to cultivate a culture in our families where we encourage growth by engaging in struggle. Carol Dweck calls this a "growth mindset."[7] Many parents have heard that we should not praise our kids for their achievements but for their effort. This advice comes in part from Carol Dweck's research—she encourages educators to support the process of struggling and encourage students when they show incremental improvement or a breakthrough to a successful outcome.

Sometimes we approach testimony with a fixed mindset, which is the tendency to accept the status quo when it comes to learning—essentially the opposite of a growth mindset. We talk about having "gained a testimony" or a pivotal experience of conversion as if it is a one-time event. However, Elder Bednar taught, "Testimony is the beginning of and a prerequisite to continuing conversion. . . . Line upon line, precept upon precept, gradually and almost imperceptibly, our motives, our thoughts, our words, and our deeds become aligned with the will of God. Conversion unto the Lord requires

---

5. D&C 88:11
6. Personal Progress was the prior youth goal setting program for Young Women. The new program, Children and Youth, encourages Personal Development goals which could include larger projects like the one mentioned here.
7. Dweck, C. S. (2006). *Mindset: The new psychology of success*. Random House Incorporated.

both persistence and patience."[8] Notice the growth mindset—effort is required for spiritual growth.

In a devotional to the students at BYU Idaho, Sheri Dew invited students to "engage in the wrestle." She urged personal growth saying, "We don't have to have answers to every question in order to receive a witness, bear witness, and stand as a witness. But questions, especially tough ones, propel us to engage in a spiritual wrestle so that the Lord can lead us along. Without plain old spiritual work, even God can't make us grow—or at least, He won't."[9] If we teach our children to have a growth mindset, questions and doubts will not be as overwhelming and scary—they will see the opportunity to learn and grow.

Finally, helping our children to see their possible future selves and think through the steps to reach goals can help motivate them (and potentially alleviate some of the need to push them). This could mean brainstorming possible careers for the future and then mapping out the steps to reach each goal. Let's take a look at how this might help to motivate a young person. One young deacon loved cars—he thought about being a mechanic, an engineer, owning a shop, or becoming a professional race car driver. He hoped to buy an old car before he turned 16 and fix it up. When scout camp came around, he was hesitant to go. His parents asked him what kind of car he thought he would try to buy—he was enthusiastic about old '70s models. Then they asked him what type of job he would get to pay for a car—he named a few of his favorite fast-food restaurants. "Did you realize," they asked, "that your scout leaders could be important references to get your first job?" He was stunned. "Can't you guys be my references?" he asked his parents. After they explained that references always come from outside the family, he saw his relationship with scout leaders in a new light (or rather two headlights and a horn). Putting bad puns aside, the point is that adolescents don't always make the connection between their everyday responsibilities and their future possibilities. If we can help make the steps concrete, we are helping them learn to use

---

8. Bednar, D. A. (2012). Converted unto the Lord. General Conference, Oct.
9. Dew, S. (2016). Will you engage in the wrestle? https://www.byui.edu/devotionals/sheri-dew

their newly developing skills of strategic thinking. When they make those connections, they are more likely to push themselves forward.

WHEN TEENAGERS PULL AWAY

One of the hardest experiences for a parent is the feeling of loss when a teenager pulls away. As parents we invest everything we have from the time our little people come into the world—sleepless nights, countless meals, bandaged knees, homework support, and family nights. When teenagers make decisions that seem to take them away from the dreams and hopes we have for their happiness, it's painful in a visceral way. And yet, we know that learning to successfully make their own decisions is the goal of parenting. How will they learn to use their agency unless they are gradually given opportunities to use it?

When we are trying to assist a struggling child, remember the lesson that Elder Uchtdorf taught about the limits of faith. He said, "Faith *is* powerful, and it often does result in miracles. But no matter how much faith we have . . . it cannot violate another person's agency."[10] To take away another's agency would violate growth and experience that enable us to develop. Each adolescent needs to learn to make his or her own decisions and mistakes as they approach adulthood.

That doesn't mean we don't set boundaries and rules for our children. Adolescents need and crave guidance (even if they don't readily accept your wisdom). Joseph Smith's example of leadership also applies to parenting as children approach adulthood: "I teach them correct principles and they govern themselves."[11] We do that through example and by finding teachable moments.

At different ages, teaching looks different. Sometimes scholars who study development compare the role that parents and teachers have to the construction of a building. We build scaffolding for our children as they grow. As a building goes up, scaffolding provides support in teachable moments—we invite kids to stretch beyond their comfort zone, but we are there to support their efforts and encourage they take risks. When they are young, we stay close, we provide

---

10. Uchtdorf, D. F. (2016). Fourth floor, last door. General Conference, Oct.
11. Packer, B. K. (1990). Teach them correct principles. General Conference, Apr.

consequences when needed. As they get older, we let them experience consequences of their actions more often and provide emotional support. Focusing on keeping a strong relationship with our children is critical for them to feel like they can come to us when they make a mistake or have a challenge. By the time they leave the house, the goal is to have removed all of the scaffolding and to continue a strong mutual relationship of support and love.

GRADUALLY RELEASING RATHER THAN PLAYING TUG-O-WAR

As a parent when we try to pull our children in one direction, sometimes we then experience their pull for independence in our lives. When do we let them pull? When do we let go just a little so they can learn on their own? Every child is different. Every situation is different. Every parent will need to stay close to the Spirit and seek guidance on this journey. We offer a couple principles to consider: First, ultimatums create no-win situations, so it's best to avoid them. For example, if parents threaten that a teenager will be grounded for two weeks if a daughter is dressing immodestly, the situation might quickly escalate to a place the parents don't want it to go. The issue becomes about control—if the parents give in, they lose credibility. Incremental consequences are better than large-scale threats. Perhaps instead, parents cancel a magazine subscription or take away her smart phone for 24 hours. Second, we recommend gradually releasing control in teen's lives guided by the principle "Where much is given, much is required."[12] For example, each year that teens get the privilege to stay up later, they might also have more responsibility around the house. We would like to explore some areas with the idea that the ultimate goal is for children to choose responsibly on their own as they approach adulthood. Where do we release? Modesty at some point, social media at some point, budgeting at some point. Ultimately, responsibility for church activity and education.

---

12. Luke 12: 29; D&C 82:3; Packer, B., K. (1974). Where much is given, much is required. General Conference, Oct.

LEARNING RESPONSIBILITY

Our hope is that when our teens leave the house, they can budget their money, do their own shopping, and manage their online presence. When they are 12 or 13, we don't always think about teaching them explicitly how to budget or protect their privacy online. Even if we do give them sound advice, do we give them a little room to practice these skills on their own? To learn from their own mistakes?

In the last couple of years before they leave the house (and to a limited extent before that), do they have a chance to be responsible for their own clothing choices? Their own money and their own bank accounts? Their own calendar and time management? Their own social media accounts? The book *The Parenting Breakthrough* by Merrilee Browne Boyack has a lot of great ideas on scaffolding responsibility.[13] For example, she recommends setting aside specific time when kids are younger to train them on specific tasks. When her children turned 12, they sat down together and made a clothing budget based on needs (not wants) and used Walmart or Target as a price guide. The choice of how to spend that money was theirs—if they wanted one expensive name brand shirt instead of three shirts, they could do that. If they wanted to save some of the money, they could do that as well. If they wanted to maximize their dollars, they learned to shop sales and buy good quality, off-brand outfits. This approach also takes the pressure off the parent-child relationship, because when a child begs for a special piece of clothing, it is their decision.

EDUCATION

Cultivating a love of learning in our youth and a desire for education may at times require some pushing and at times releasing. What are some areas that are helpful to push teens when it comes to education? As parents we can help our youth understand the importance of education. The importance of learning is embedded in the doctrinal DNA of the gospel. We have been encouraged to "seek ye diligently and teach one another words of wisdom; . . . seek learning, even by

---

13. Browne Boyack, M. (2005). *The parenting breakthrough: A real-life plan to teach your kids to work, save money, and be truly independent.* Salt Lake City, UT: Deseret Book.

study and also by faith. . . . . [E]stablish a house, even a house of prayer, a house of fasting, a house of faith, a house of learning, a house of glory, a house of order, a house of God."[14] In addition to a love of learning, we can talk to our children about investing wisely in education as a practical approach to career preparation. We can help them understand that in the US we face a shortage of skilled workers. For example, in 2016, researchers reported that 500,000 computer and IT jobs were vacant. We may encourage them to take career preparation courses that help them understand their strengths and passions and then find mentored internship experiences to try out possible career paths.

Another way we can support education is to help them understand the systems of education. If you don't understand what they need to graduate from high school and college, assist them in finding mentors who do. Jessica shares that as a first-generation college student, she was sent on a plane to her first semester alone. She says, "I knew no one and had little information about the way college worked. I don't really remember how I got from the plane, to the bus station, to my apartment. I chose the cheapest apartment far from campus and stores. The night I landed, I remember calling my parents crying because the fridge was moldy, the apartment was awful, and I was unsure about my choice and roommates. Thankfully, I grew to love my roommates. I landed in a class that taught me how to create a graduation plan, create short- and long-term goals, and succeed in college. I learned that I could take 12 or 22 credits and the cost of living and credits were equal. I chose 22 and graduated in three semesters and a summer course with my associate degree. I didn't start in a place where support was readily available, but I fell into a place of support."

Jen was also the first one in her family to go away for college; however, her experience was different. When she was preparing to leave for college, parents of a close friend took her under their wing. They invited her to join them on a family vacation, got her oriented to the university the week before school started, and helped her set up her dorm room. Both of these are stories about developing independence, but in both cases, support from adults in the form of a class or a form of mentors was critical. Encouraging our youth to

---

14. D&C 88:118–119

connect with support resources outside of the family is an important skill to thrive in education.

For high-achieving youth, our job may be to encourage them to unstring the bow and relax their expectations once in a while. As parents, we may need to release our own anxiety in order to help our kids release their anxiety. Part of releasing our anxiety is encouraging them to avoid perfectionism and learn that failing is part of the process. In a commencement address for his son's 8th grade graduating class, Supreme Court Justice Roberts gave an unconventional message. Rather than wishing the graduates luck and success, he said, "From time to time in the years to come, I hope you will be treated unfairly, so that you will come to know the value of justice. I hope that you will suffer betrayal because that will teach you the importance of loyalty. Sorry to say, but I hope you will be lonely from time to time so that you don't take friends for granted. I wish you bad luck, again, from time to time so that you will be conscious of the role of chance in life and understand that your success is not completely deserved and that the failure of others is not completely deserved either."[15]

Another example where we can and should help our kids learn to avoid perfectionism and keep doors open is the college search. The book *Where You Go Is Not Who You'll Be: An Antidote to the College Admissions Mania* is a great read for parents and adolescents who feel the pressure to perform for the pending college applications.[16] In the opening chapter, the authors focus on success stories of famous people who didn't go to Ivy League schools such as Doug McMillon, the CEO at Walmart who went to the University of Arkansas, President Joe Biden who went to the University of Delaware, Ronald Regan who when to Eureka College in Illinois, or Pulitzer prize winner David Kocieniewski who went to State University at New York at Binghamton. Others, like Governor Joe Christie or Forbes 30 under 30 honoree Isaac Kinde attribute at least part of their success to not getting into their top choice for college. From those experiences, they

15. Reilly, Katie. (5 July 2017). "I wish you bad luck. Read Supreme Court Justice John Roberts unconventional speech to his son's graduating class." *Time*. http://time.com/4845150/chief-justice-john-roberts-commencement-speech-transcript/.

16. Bruni, F. (2015). *Where You Go Is Not Who You'll Be: An Antidote to the College Admissions Mania*. New York: Grand Central Publishing.

learned grit, the value of support systems, networking, and the importance of struggle.

As parents, we may also believe that a four-year degree is for everyone, but that is not necessarily the case. According to the census, about 33% of adults have a four-year degree.[17] Drawbacks to getting a four-year degree have been highlighted in recent years, including high cost and debt (on average 37k for college grads in 2016), potentially irrelevant knowledge when technology is changing so quickly, and unpredictable job markets.[18] In a longitudinal study, those who had a four-year degree weathered the Great Recession fairly well. Those who had a two-year degree also rode the storm out fairly well. Skilled workers with a certificate had a harder time, and those without education suffered the most.[19] The message here is that two-year degrees may be a stable alternative for many of our youth if a four-year degree feels overwhelming. Pursuing a two-year degree as a stepping-stone to further education may also be a way of minimizing debt.

Education seems to improve social outcomes—from teen pregnancy, to financial stability, to low drug and alcohol consumption.[20] Some evidence even suggests that parental education protects against depression and low self-esteem in the next generation.[21] So yes, education is incredibly important, financially, socially, and spiritually; however, as parents we can help our children recognize that there are different ways to obtaining education. The Pathways Connection program, sponsored by the Church through BYU Idaho provides one way of obtaining a degree online while providing face-to-face

---

17. United States Census Bureau. (30 March 2017). Highest educational levels reached by adults in the U.S. Since 1940. https://www.census.gov/newsroom/press-releases/2017/cb17-51.html.

18. Mortimer, J. & Tjaden, J. (Oct. 2016). Higher education, school-to-work transition, and future prospects: Converging challenges in the U.S. and Germany. Society for Longitudinal and Life Course Studies, Bamberg.

19. Vuolo, M., Mortimer, J. T., & Staff, J. (2016). The value of educational degrees in turbulent economic times: Evidence from the Youth Development Study. *Social Science Research*, *57*, 233–252.

20. Putnam, R. D. (2016). *Our kids: The American dream in crisis*. New York: Simon & Schuster.

21. Staff, J., Doty, J. L., Wu, C., Mortimer, J., & Johnson, M. K. (Apr. 2015). Parental education and child wellbeing: A prospective longitudinal study. Paper presented at the Population Association of America, San Diego, CA.

support.[22] Regardless of the path our children choose, we can encourage education while supporting the growing autonomy of our children.

FINDING BALANCE

For parents in particular, it seems like we tend to get mixed messages simultaneously telling us to push our kids and pull back. Jessica recently went to an eighth-grade orientation meeting. She says, "I was told about the format of each class. Each teacher was careful to point out the need to download the app that will help me to track my son's progress. I was told by six teachers that if I am conscientious, follow my son's homework and missing assignments, I can help him to be successful." It is curious that as parents we are often shamed for "helicoptering" or trying to control our children versus teaching them to be successful adults and independent. In the same breath, we are also given the message that we are responsible for school and other successes. That mixed message can be confusing and frustrating. It makes push and release a balancing act that cannot be done perfectly. Further, if your child has a personality or diagnosis that makes organization and "keeping track of things" difficult, you may feel the need to key into the many resources to push your child forward in education. Supporting other's efforts and resisting the temptation to force your way of doing things on others is essential in creating good support networks as parents.

In sum, as parents we need to learn to be flexible about when we push and don't push. Jessica spoke with a mission president's wife who perfectly addressed one challenge with pushing and pulling. She talked about the irony associated with putting a group of sisters and elders in a room and both encouraging them to do better and try harder while also asking them to be compassionate and gentle with themselves. She said the elders and sisters who were struggling with rules and following through would inevitably hear the message that they should be compassionate and gentle with themselves. While those missionaries who were already feeling anxious about their performance and were

---

22. https://byupathway.lds.org/

struggling with self-compassion would feel increasingly overwhelmed by the message to try harder, be more obedient and do better. In other words, a one size fits all approach to working with our youth often doesn't work. In parenting and in mentoring, knowing the individual needs of our young people is critical. Keep track of what seems to be working best for your child and ask for feedback from your child and those that might be trying to help them. When you think you've got a good balance of pushing, you may need to adjust. Perhaps you may feel that your child needs consistent pushing and when you ask a therapist, your child, or a trusted confidant they may encourage you to push less or more. Experimenting with options and being prepared to adjust in the future will help you and your child find balance.

CHAPTER ⑥

Promoting Spirituality of Our Youth

When it comes to promoting spirituality, most of us know the importance of the basics. The small and simple habits of personal prayer and scripture reading are critical for youth to develop their own testimonies. Family habits of scripture study, gathering to say prayers, and weekly church attendance are also critical. President Nelson has taught us that as we focus on making our homes centers of gospel learning, we can "unleash the power of families, as each family follows through conscientiously and carefully to transform their home into a sanctuary of faith."[1] In an increasingly secular world, where spirituality and religious observance are frequently mocked, the basics are the foundation for spiritual growth.

Another critical layer is creating an atmosphere where teens can ask questions and honestly talk through their doubts while getting support for faith. Eventually, we want to teach our children the process of how to find deeply personal answers. In seminary a few years ago, students were taught a simple process that lays the groundwork

---

1. Nelson, R. M. (2018). Becoming Exemplary Latter-day Saints. General Conference, Oct.

for finding answers, Acquiring Spiritual Knowledge (ASK).[2] ASK includes three principles to guide young people in seeking answers:

1. Act in Faith.

Developmentally, teenagers are prone to see things in black and white, all wrong or all right. When they run up against something that doesn't make sense to them, it can be tempting to throw away their whole testimony. This principle encourages them to hang in there and not hang up their faith. As Elder Holland taught, "When those moments come and issues surface, the resolution of which is not immediately forthcoming, *hold fast to what you already know and stand strong until additional knowledge comes.*"[3] As parents, we can encourage youth to walk in faith and express confidence that as they do, they will receive a testimony. We can also teach them that faith does not mean knowing everything. As Alma taught, faith implies not knowing. Once we learn something for ourselves, "[o]ur faith is dormant,"[4] but in the meantime, faith requires stepping forward even when we have questions or gaps in our testimonies.

2. Examine questions from an eternal perspective.

This means that we teach our kids to think about things from the perspective of the plan of salvation—to look at the big picture. It also means that we check ourselves to see if we are thinking about things from a worldly point of view. For example, as a researcher, Jen knows that sleep is crucial for adolescents and that teenagers' sleep rhythms tend toward late nights rather than early mornings. From a strictly academic perspective, early morning seminary doesn't benefit adolescents. On the other hand, having taught seminary, she also has seen the spiritual benefit of when adolescents make the sacrifice to go to seminary. So, as a parent, she has encouraged a healthy balance of getting to bed at a decent hour, encouraging her teenagers to attend seminary, and appreciating the flexibility of make-up lessons. From an eternal perspective, seminary attendance isn't necessary for salvation, but going provides key support for building testimony and protection

---

2. The Church of Jesus Christ of Latter-day Saints. (2017). Acquiring Spiritual Knowledge. *Doctrinal Mastery Book of Mormon Teacher Manual.* Salt Lake City, UT.

3. Holland, J. R. (2013). "Lord, I Believe." General Conference, Apr.

4. Alma 32:34

from a tough environment during the high school years and helps adolescents walk the covenant path.

3. Seek further understanding through divinely appointed sources.

President Nelson has emphasized direct revelation as the ultimate source of truth.[5] Personal revelation often requires searching out answers in the divinely appointed sources, including scriptures and words of apostles and prophets. In contrast, Generation Z, who are ages 5–25 in 2020, has been raised with extensive access to the Internet. This is a generation that are considered "digital natives." They are used to getting information from their favorite Youtubers or Buzzfeed. In a pop-culture environment that has grown increasingly cynical and secular, as parents we need to encourage our youth to seek spiritual answers in places that support and nurture a relationship with our Heavenly Father.

Ultimately, we need to teach our children to ask Heavenly Father directly for divine revelation and how to recognize answers. In a devotional at BYU Idaho, Sister Sheri Dew described that when young people approach her with questions, she asks, "Are you willing to engage in the wrestle? In an ongoing spiritual wrestle?" She explained, "Spiritual wrestling leverages the strength of true doctrine to overpower our weaknesses, our wavering faith, and our lack of knowledge. Spiritual wrestlers are seekers. They are men and women of faith who want to understand more than they presently do and who are serious about increasing the light and knowledge in their lives." Her full talk is an excellent resource for parents to read with their adolescents.[6]

Another related principle that is helpful to teach our children is that God will not always give us clear guidance on every decision when we ask for help. Sometimes He gives us the growth experience of taking a few steps on our own in the dark.[7] In her own words, Jessica describes how she experienced this phenomenon: "Recently we were in the process of making a large financial decision. Not knowing

---

5. Nelson, R. M. (2018). Revelation for the Church, Revelation for Our Lives. General Conference, Apr.

6. Dew, S. (2016). Will you engage in the wrestle? https://www.byui.edu/devotionals/sheri-dew.

7. Packer, B. K. (Jan. 1982). Candle of the Lord. *Ensign*.

which way is the 'right way to go' is difficult and daunting. I wanted a clear answer from God about what to do. Instead, my answer was a feeling that it would be okay and that I would make decisions with both positive and negative consequences." We need to teach our children that Heavenly Father does not always guide us clearly to know exactly which way to go. That was Satan's plan—we would have clear direction, and we would all return to our Heavenly Father. Instead, Heavenly Father wants us to learn from our choices (positive and negative) and grow. Because we hear so many wonderful talks about promptings, we sometimes develop what psychologists call "magical thinking," a belief that insight into the way to go will be given at every turn. If our youth only have that perspective, they can feel they either don't receive inspiration or that God has abandoned them when He is teaching them to make decisions. We can reinforce this by letting them make decisions from the time they are small and helping them to lovingly deal with the consequences (keeping in check the "I told you so" tone).

We also need to be careful when our own doubt or cynicism pops up. Elder Holland taught a lesson that applies here. In a 2003 talk, entitled "A Prayer for the Children," he said, "In matters of religion a skeptical mind is not a higher manifestation of virtue than is a believing heart, and analytical deconstruction in the field of, say, literary fiction can be just plain old-fashioned destruction when transferred to families yearning for faith at home."[8] These ideas extend to the practice of faith and hope. Think about the time it takes a child to build a tower with blocks—sometimes the better part of an hour. How long does it take for a two-year-old to come by and raze the tower? Ten seconds, or less. The same is true of faith and doubt—it takes time and patience to build faith, and some delight in tearing faith down because it is easy and has a dramatic effect that creates buzz on social media. In contrast, when communities work to build faith together over time, everyone benefits.

---

8. Holland, J. R. (2003). A Prayer for the Children. General Conference, Apr.

PARENTING AND BUILDING SPIRITUALITY

Parenting is often intertwined with the process of youth developing a relationship with God. Our faith in Heavenly Father is a gift we as Latter-day Saint parents actively seek to share with our children. Defining a relationship with the divine more broadly, Lisa Miller and colleagues found that shared sense of spirituality passed from generation to generation was a strong protection against depression, alcohol use, and harmful risk taking.[9] They found that among families who were at high risk for depression, when parents and youth shared a sense of spirituality, they were 80% less likely to experience depression than those who did not.[10] Shared spirituality across three generations—child, parent, and grandparents—had an even stronger protective effect. Depression was 90% less likely. Practicing spirituality isn't a fail-safe, and many of us need professional help at one point in our lives, but practicing spirituality builds a layer of emotional protection.

In several studies, one group of researchers found that children tended to take characteristics they see in their parents and apply them to their relationship with a higher power.[9] In other words, if their parents are harsh and easily dole out punishment, children are more likely to develop a view of God as harsh and punitive. If parents are understanding yet firm, then children are more likely to develop a view of God as merciful and just. As a friend posted recently on Facebook in memory of her father, "Because of the unconditional love of my father, I find it easy to believe that I have a Heavenly Father who also loves me unconditionally."[11]

When Jen saw this research, she felt a bit overwhelmed—that is a huge responsibility. For all of us who are feeling overwhelmed or guilty, especially when our children struggle (or we struggle with our children), here is an important sidenote on research findings. Most research reports averages. So, on average strong parent-child relationships contribute to a better relationship with Heavenly Father. But

---

9. Miller, L. (2016). *The spiritual child: The new science on parenting for health and lifelong thriving*. New York: Macmillan.

10. Miller, L., Warner, V., Wickramaratne, P., & Weissman, M. (1997). Religiosity and depression: Ten-year follow-up of depressed mothers and offspring. *Journal of the American Academy of Child & Adolescent Psychiatry, 36*(10), 1416–1425.

11. Flake, L. 2008. Facebook post. Used with permission.

there are so many variables that contribute—personality, personal choices, peers, culture, and experiences at church. The list goes on and on, and the research finding doesn't apply to everyone. Some of the most faithful, best parents we know have children who don't share their faith.

In contrast, other research found that youth who did not have a close relationship with parents were protected from risk when they developed a close relationship with God. They seemed to find the warmth and nurturing from a spiritual relationship that many others found in their parental relationships.[9] There are youth whose parents are not in the picture or who are abusive or neglectful. For these kids, building a loving relationship with God may fill the gap of parenting—teens in this type of situation who reported a relationship with a higher being had better outcomes than those who didn't.[9] Our past stake president, Scott Naatjes, reminded us that our lives may be difficult, but they are always better with the gospel than without. Children who have been given the gift of the gospel and taught how to have a personal, redemptive relationship with Heavenly Father are better off, no matter what their current circumstances.

STRUGGLES WITH CHURCH ACTIVITY

When our children resist participating in church activities, sometimes it is helpful to push our teenagers to attend church activities, and sometimes it is not—we often learn this is trial by error. If you push your child to attend church, while they are there, they may feel a spark that helps them or brush shoulders with leaders that love them. The opposite can also be true. Sometimes pushing leads to a youth pulling away from parents and the teachings of the gospel. In other words, if you asked us if you should make your 17-year-old child go to church, the best answer we have is to counsel with your child, your leaders, and pray about it. Because churches are composed of congregations full of imperfect people, at some point most churchgoers will likely be either offended or uplifted, and probably both over time. Anytime people come together in a community, we all play a role in strengthening and weakening relationships. No person can be a perfect leader or friend to every person within a large community.

A developmental task most teenagers work through during middle school into young adulthood is "differentiation," according to developmental and identity theorists.[12] In other words, they may try to find their own identity by doing things differently than their mom and dad. Given that, if your teen is struggling to create identity and individuality, they may differentiate themselves from you by making choices contrary to your way of thinking, such as refusing to go to church or challenging aspects of the gospel. They may want to argue about aspects of church doctrine. Often, one of the worst things we can do is engage in an argument and try to convince our youth that they are wrong. Instead, youth feel respected and taken seriously when we listen to their questions, encourage them to seek answers to their questions, and read faith-building talks with them like "Engage in the Wrestle."[6] If they are differentiating, youth will likely look for and find the weaknesses in your branch or ward. They may look for every opportunity to resist attending activities and Sunday services.

When a teenager resists attendance, here are some possible strategies. Begin by considering the age of the youth. It may be appropriate to insist that younger youth attend, firmly but calmly sending the message that "These are our family's expectations." For older youth, perhaps consider compromising on some activities—maybe it's not necessary that they attend the ward Christmas party or girls' camp. One active member of the Church, a mother with young children, explained that she was grateful her mother recognized that camping was not among her strengths and did not force her to go to girls' camp. Perhaps an exchange can be negotiated—for example, instead of going to the service project, let's go on a ministering visit, which would accomplish some of the same goals of serving others and connecting the youth to the ward family. Perhaps a youth about to graduate could

---

12. According to these therapists, differentiation implies being separate but maintaining emotional connections. Evidence has demonstrated that having a balance between personal identity and emotional ties with others is a healthy pathway of development.
    Bowen, M. (1978). Jenkins, S. M., Buboltz, W. C., Schwartz, J. P., & Johnson, P. (2005). Differentiation of self and psychosocial development. *Contemporary Family Therapy, 27*(2), 251–261.

participate in a nearby YSA branch if they don't feel comfortable in their own ward. For those who are struggling with more severe challenges, perhaps with depression or anxiety, try to identify baseline experiences—maybe the youth at least attends temple trips or at least stays for sacrament meeting—and celebrate what they are able to do in times of struggle.

When Jen was teaching seminary, she and her husband had to make a difficult decision about their daughter's attendance. She tells the story here in her own words: "One of our children was struggling with anxiety, and as a result, she was getting very little sleep and her anxiety was growing out of control. When it started to spiral into a severe depression, we sought out professional help. Not surprisingly, one of the first things the therapist suggested was that she drop seminary. We let our daughter make the decision but encouraged her to attend when she felt she was able. This was painful, because at the time I taught seminary in our very own basement, and I was pouring my heart and soul into teaching those kids every morning. I had to swallow my pride and not compare my daughter to the other kids who found a way to drag themselves out of bed and into frigid Minnesota temperatures to study the scriptures. Sometimes I felt inspired to include something for her, but then she wasn't there. I was making a sacrifice that seemed to be benefiting other people's children but hurting my own. But if we had to make that decision again, I think we would do the same thing. She needed space, healing, and rest.

This experience was a lesson to me about my own pride—our practice of the gospel is personal, not about what other people think or earning points to heaven with our efforts. In fact, when my daughter read this book, she noticed that this story was missing, and she encouraged me to include it. I had wanted to protect her privacy, and maybe, just maybe, there was some of that old pride sticking around. She insisted, though, that difficult, raw experiences are among the most valuable to share. I'm grateful for her honest heart, her courage to keep getting up when life knocks her down, and her willingness to share."

An important principle in all of this is to avoid a pattern of coercion or making youth attend activities and worship by force and power, which may do more harm than good. Doctrine and Covenants 121:41 reminds us that "No power or influence can or ought to be maintained by virtue of the priesthood, only by persuasion, by long-suffering, by gentleness and meekness, and by love unfeigned," which is also good parenting advice. Research has documented that parental coercion leads to youth seeking out negative friendships, and in turn, youth may learn delinquent behaviors from a negative peer group.[13] In other words, parental coercion may set off a negative spiral.

One last thought: When our youth are struggling spiritually or having a hard time engaging in church activity, the basic patterns of living the gospel at home are gold. Sister Linda Reeves, the second counselor in the General Relief Society, testified of the "blessings of daily scripture study and prayer and weekly family home evening. These are the very practices that help take away stress, give direction to our lives, and add protection to our homes."[14] When parents with young children wrestle to establish gospel habits, it may not feel like the daily struggle is worth it, but the payoff often comes in the teenage years. This is exactly where the new Children and Youth program can be critically important.

If a child is struggling with church activity, having those habits ingrained into daily home life can be a spiritual lifeline. Parents will have built-in opportunities to offer spiritual nourishment during times when teens may need daily support. Especially for teenagers, the ability to counsel with parents—whether one-on-one or all together in a more formal family meeting—is another lifeline. Elder Ballard promised, "A family council that is patterned after the councils in heaven, filled with Christlike love, and guided by the Lord's Spirit will help us to protect our family. . . . Combined with prayer, a family council will invite the presence of the Savior, as He promised: 'For where two or three are gathered together in my name, there am I in the midst of them.'"[15] Additionally, teenagers can have a place where their voices are heard and their opinions are validated. That doesn't mean that parents will always agree with them, but they can know that they are understood and valued.

---

13. Patterson, G. R. (2016). Coercion theory. In T. J. Dishion & J. Snyder (Eds.), *The Oxford Handbook of Coercive Relationship Dynamics* (Vol. 1). New York, NY: Oxford University Press. doi:10.1093/oxfordhb/9780199324552.013.2.

14. Reeves, L. S. (2014). Protection from Pornography—A Christ-Focused Home. General Conference, Apr.

15. Ballard, M. R. (2016). Family Councils. General Conference, Apr.

TAKING THE LONG VIEW OF SPIRITUAL DEVELOPMENT

Jessica recently attended a multi-stake youth conference. She was told at the orientation to "love the youth. Don't look at their outward appearance and avoid criticizing their choices." This led to an ease in connecting to youth who otherwise may not have come to the conference. Some youth hadn't kept the dress standards perfectly, and some were involved in their cell phones more than each other. The person outlining the rules said, "They signed an agreement about the rules, and they know what the standards are. Allow them to govern themselves." Jessica said, "I have often been the person to tell people to put their cell phones away or to gently criticize a choice. Being at the conference, I realized that the only long-term change that policing youth's choices really promotes is distrust within the relationship between leader and youth." Similarly, a parent certainly needs to set boundaries and enforce them with consequences. However, care should be given that youth are able to feel the weight of their own decisions without shame from others. If shame is felt acutely, it blocks natural consequences for the actions.

Sometimes, we all have to struggle with our own sense of failure and shame. When we feel guilty as parents because of our faults, mistakes, and weaknesses, we can find peace remembering that the Lord's acceptance of imperfect parents is a theme of the Old Testament. In particular, as mothers, we may be drawn to the stories of imperfect women, who make mistakes yet manage to have faith. Perhaps Matthew, the writer of the gospel of Matthew, reflects a similar respect for these women of faith when he lists Christ's genealogy at the beginning of his account. Although they are not all named, the list includes:

- Sarah, who doubted she could have a child and even laughed at the thought.
- Leah, Jacob's second choice, who may have always felt like she was in Rachel's shadow.
- Tamar, who was determined to be a mother by means we tend to find questionable today.

- Rahab, a Canaanite woman who is labeled a harlot, but saves Israelite spies and may have been the first convert to the Jewish faith.
- Ruth, a Moabite woman, who understood what it was like to be a stranger.
- Bathsheba, the mother of Soloman, who had an affair with the king (though we might wonder if she felt her choices were limited).
- Mary, herself, Jesus Christ's mother, who must have had to endure the shaming glances from others that did not believe the story of His conception.

In Hebrews, as the epistle writer gives concrete examples of faith, trying to help make the concept more tangible, Sarah is remembered for her faith despite the improbability of having a child, and Rahab is remembered for believing when no one else around her believed.[16] If Christ chose these women to claim as his mother and great-grandmothers, what does that say of our imperfections? Isn't it possible that they be swallowed up in His love as we continuously return to Him in faith?

In the end, once we have taught our children the best way we know how, we have to let go. Agency is a principle that we fought a war to win in the premortal life. We have to ask ourselves if we truly believe in the eternal plan that we have taught them. If we do, taking the long view will be easier. Orson F. Whitney shared a teaching that may bring some comfort, "The Prophet Joseph Smith declared—and he never taught a more comforting doctrine—that the eternal sealings of faithful parents and the divine promises made to them for valiant service in the Cause of Truth, would save not only themselves, but likewise their posterity. Though some of the sheep may wander, the eye of the Shepherd is upon them, and sooner or later they will feel the tentacles of Divine Providence reaching out after them and drawing them back to the fold."[17]

---

16. Hebrews 11:11, 31
17. Hope for Parents of Wayward Children. (Sept. 2002) *Ensign*.

More recently, Boyd K. Packer taught:

The measure of our success as parents . . . will not rest solely on how our children turn out. That judgment would be just only if we could raise our families in a perfectly moral environment, and that now is not possible.

It is not uncommon for responsible parents to lose one of their children, for a time, to influences over which they have no control. They agonize over rebellious sons or daughters. They are puzzled over why they are so helpless when they have tried so hard to do what they should. . . .

We cannot overemphasize the value of temple marriage, the binding ties of the sealing ordinance, and the standards of worthiness required of them. When parents keep the covenants, they have made at the altar of the temple, their children will be forever bound to them.[18]

Having an eternal perspective, helps us put our worry on the shelf and trust the Lord instead of emotionally being "like a wave of the sea driven with the wind and tossed."[19]

Focusing on strengthening our own personal relationship with God and having a healthy relationship with our children may be the best gift we can give as they transition to adulthood. Our lives speak louder than our lectures or even our advice as we joyfully, humbly live the gospel and let the Lord work in us to become our best selves. What daily practices help us in that journey? When we model healthy coping, spiritual development, and balance in our own lives, we are teaching powerful lessons to our children about finding these qualities in their lives as well. In essence, we believe that one of the best ways to teach resilience to our youth is to practice resilience ourselves. With this in mind, we turn to the two most basic commandments as taught by Christ: Love the Lord your God with all your heart, mind, and strength (Ch. 7) and love your neighbor as yourself (Ch. 8).

---

18. Packer, B. K. (1992). Our Moral Environment. General Conference, Apr.
19. James 1:6

PART ❸

Being Spiritually Grounded as Parents of Youth

CHAPTER **7**

Practicing Healthy Habits of the Heart by Loving God

Why would we focus on parents' spiritual habits in a book about practicing resilience and parenting adolescents? First, as youth are preparing for adulthood, our actions often speak louder than words. Letting our children see the gospel active in our daily lives as we practice spiritually rich and authentic living may be the most powerful lesson we can teach our children about building resilience. For many parents whose children are struggling spiritually, the way we live may be the only sermon our youth hear.

Second, being spiritually grounded will help us stay anchored when the storms come. As Helaman taught his sons, "Remember, remember, that it is upon the rock of our Redeemer, who is Christ, the Son of God, that ye must build your foundation; that when the devil shall send forth his mighty winds, yea, his shafts in the whirlwind, yea, when all his hail and his mighty storm shall beat upon you, it shall have no power over you to drag you down."[1] Notice that the verse doesn't say "if" storms come, but "when." In other words, when

---

1. Helaman 5:12

we are personally grounded in a strong foundation, we are prepared to teach our youth to build their foundation.

Third, intentionally choosing and building daily habits makes everything else run smoother, including parenting, and in turn, we can help our youth be thoughtful about their own daily habits. The hope is that we can pass on the faith and wisdom of generations to our children.

Fourth, when we focus on our relationship with Heavenly Father, we can feel strength. Turning to Him is something we have control over. He is the perfect parent and always reaches toward us. In turn, we can improve our side of the relationship. This is especially helpful when things are difficult in other relationships.

Some memories stay with us for life, like a clear picture lit by a camera flash—for Jen, one of these came right before she got married. She remembers hanging out with her dad one evening: "I asked him if he had any advice for me before getting married, and I thought he would have a long list of guidance for me. Instead, he summed it all up with two guiding principles:

- 'Love the Lord your God with all [your] heart, with all [your] soul, and with all [your] mind.'
- And 'Love your neighbor as yourself.'[2]

I've never forgotten that—and when life gets hectic and complicated, it's helpful to go back to the simple and profound guideposts that the Savior gave us that my dad passed on to me."

When it comes to the first commandment to love the Lord, nourishing our relationship with God can get lost in the pressure of everyday tasks in our busy lives. But this is a relationship that will strengthen our ability to get through daily life and give us perspective when we would get caught in the weeds on our own. Consciously, we need to make the choice to establish habits that put God first. Elder Uchtdorf refers to this as being intentional.[3] Our habits are developed as our thought patterns become established as neural pathways in our brain.

---

2. Matthew 22:36–40
3. Uchtdorf, D. F. (2019). Your Great Adventure. General Conference, Oct.

Once habits are established, it takes less effort to carry through.[4] For adults many of these patterns are well-established habits, but studies like the one we discussed in Chapter 3 that set up a loving kindness intervention show that habits of the heart can be changed for the better. When our minds literally get stuck in a rut, we can consciously take steps to establish better emotional and thought habits.[5] We can start by establishing habits that connect us with our Heavenly Father.

DEVELOPING HABITS OF THE HEART

Alma teaches his son the importance of spiritual, daily habits when he says, "[B]y small and simple things are great things brought to pass; and small means in many instances doth confound the wise."[6] There are concrete steps to establishing new habits—what we might think of as small and simple things. First, writing a weekly goal down and putting it in a visible place increases the likelihood that we will accomplish that goal. Maybe write a card with a written goal that is visible on your bed stand or mirror. Maybe use an online to-do list that sends pop-up notifications. Second, having a visual cue will kickstart the process of engaging in that habit. For example, workout clothes laid out at night can be a cue to exercise in the morning. A prayer stone on your pillow can be a reminder to pray before bed. Pairing a new habit with a well-established habit is a good strategy. Third, focus on the rewards of the habit you want to form. These might be intrinsic rewards like the satisfaction of sending off a note to someone as part of our ministering efforts or taking a few minutes to enjoy peace and quiet after a prayer. The lesson here is that focusing on the process of setting up a desired habit will go a long way toward the success of making it a long-term part of our lives.

After a while, the habits become automatic and require less effort. Think of little children learning to tie their shoes. They struggle with

---

4. Duhigg, C. (2012). *The power of habit: Why we do what we do in life and business.* Random House. This is a great resource for thinking about how to systematically set up habits in your life!
5. Hanson, R. (2009). *Buddha's brain: The practical neuroscience of happiness, love, and wisdom.* New Harbinger Publications.
6. Alma 37:6

every step of the process—they have to think through the position of their hands and the way that the string goes around their fingers. But within a few months, it becomes much easier, and after a few years they don't think about it at all. In the same way, we can intentionally focus on habits in our personal lives and our family life that take effort at first but then become an established part of our day. It's helpful if we take our children on our journey of self-improvement. Talking to your teens about your goal setting and efforts for change helps them to see that improvement is continuous and that you are aware of your flaws, and this builds trust. It may provide a pattern for them to follow in their own goal-making in the Children and Youth program.

Positive habits have been shown to have a positive spiraling effect on other areas of life. For example, one study found that when a person begins to exercise, they also start to become more organized, get to bed on time, and wake up earlier.[4] Researchers questioned whether it was the effect of exercise or the effect of habits, so they tried experimenting with a different habit. The same spiraling positive pattern was found when participants started studying longer or when they started eating more healthfully. It was as if habits were contagious, and willpower overflowed into other areas of their lives.

If the most powerful habits are those that connect us with our Heavenly Father, what are the small and simple things in our lives that can have a rippling effect? Below, we talk about the importance of having a close relationship with God, including some research that illustrates the benefits of having this spiritual connection. Then we discuss some daily habits that help us to cultivate a relationship with our Heavenly Father.

PERSONAL RELATIONSHIP WITH GOD

A personal relationship with deity is a key to optimism. A recent line of research has found that being spiritually grounded was related to having a stronger sense of optimism and grit when times get tough.[7] In his letter to the Corinthians, Paul shared an example of this when he

---

7. Miller, L. (2016). *The spiritual child: The new science on parenting for health and lifelong thriving*. New York: Macmillan.

said that he had a "thorn in the flesh,"[8] a problem that he prayed would go away again and again. But instead, the Lord taught him, "My grace is sufficient for thee: for my strength is made perfect in weakness."[9] As we consciously build a relationship with Heavenly Father, find hope and power in the Atonement of Jesus Christ, and seek the guidance of the Spirit, we are often blessed with strength to endure.

In a general conference address, President Russell M. Nelson described the stream of messages from media and social media and stated, "[I]n coming days, it will not be possible to survive spiritually without the guiding, directing, comforting, and constant influence of the Holy Ghost."[10] It is no coincidence that in the same breath, President Nelson voiced his optimism about the future. President Nelson shared a process of receiving personal revelation for our lives and recommended making this a daily habit. Here are the steps he outlined:

1. "Find a quiet place where you can regularly go.

2. Humble yourself before God.

3. Pour out your heart to your Heavenly Father. Turn to Him for answers and for comfort.

4. Pray in the name of Jesus Christ about your concerns, your fears, your weaknesses—yes, the very longings of your heart.

5. And then listen! Write the thoughts that come to your mind. Record your feelings and follow through with actions that you are prompted to take."

President Nelson then asked, "Does God really *want* to speak to you?" And answered with a resounding "Yes!" He wants to have that personal connection with each of us.

When one of Jen's children was struggling, she and her husband felt at a loss because their child was overcommitted to good things and experiencing anxiety as a result. They were literally on their knees when an idea came to their mind to use the concept of balance and

---

8. 2 Corinthians 12:7
9. 2 Corinthians 12:9
10. Nelson, R. M. (2018). Revelation for the Church, Revelation for Our Lives. General Conference, Apr.

to visualize a mobile. This metaphor of being out-of-balance seemed to resonate with their teen and helped them strategize together to set some healthy boundaries. Later, the metaphor also helped when one of their kids felt reluctant to get involved at school, at church, and in the community. In that case, they used the metaphor to invite this child to step outside their comfort zone. To this day, they felt like that idea was a communication from God that helped them in their parenting.

MINDFULNESS AND MEDITATION

Mindfulness is a powerful practice of being in the moment, letting go of the spinning worries about tomorrow and the obsessive reviewing of the past. Mindfulness encourages us to be aware of our bodies, connect to the earth, and breathe deeply. When we are mindful, we slow down and pay attention. We also practice non-judgmental awareness of our emotions, checking in to see where we are without feeling bad if we noticed emotions that are sometimes labeled "negative."[11] When Jessica recently took a 9-week mindfulness and meditation class, the instructor stated that as negative thoughts, emotions, and even physical sensations were observed during a meditation, that the goal was to notice and then gently let them go versus judging the moment, body, or thought. As we are mindful, we practice being in the present and just acknowledging the emotions, letting them go, as if they are dancing across the stage of our mind.

In our Latter-day Saint tradition, we don't talk much about mindfulness, but we do talk of related subjects—for example pondering or meditation. In his talk, "The Race of Life," President Monson asked, "In this fast-paced life, do we ever pause for moments of meditation—even thoughts of timeless truths?"[12] He noted that when tragedy or illness strikes, often our minds become focused, and we realize what is really important. Mindfulness is a practice of clearing our minds so we can focus daily on what is really important. It doesn't displace the practice

---

11. Gallant, S. N. (2016). Mindfulness meditation practice and executive functioning: Breaking down the benefit. *Consciousness and cognition*, *40*, 116–130.
12. Monson, T. S. (2012). The Race of Life. General Conference, Apr.

of pondering, or focusing on eternal truth; in fact, meditating mindfully aids the process by slowing down and calming our active minds.

Our minds are constantly spinning, thinking, worrying, and noticing.[5] As we practice our faith in today's busy world, our desires to do good and work toward perfection might lead us to long to-do lists and worries about how much we fall short. In the past, the monotony of daily chores and closer ties to nature gave us mental space to be mindful, but in today's world technology has taken over much of the monotonous and boring tasks of the past like milking cows, walking to get water, or scrubbing clothing. Disclaimer—we absolutely don't advocate going back to those days! However, we recognize the need to learn to stand still and build mental space back into our lives—literally breathing room.

In therapy, Jessica has often suggested small and simple ways to begin mindfulness and mediation. A few techniques are:

1. Do some light stretching or yoga to relax your body. If your body is tense, it is difficult to quiet your mind.

2. An easy way to check your tension is to raise your shoulders to your ears and release them down. If you notice that there was tension or that your shoulders were closer to your ears than needed to start, then take a moment to look at your posture and tension in your body.

3. Take some deep "cleansing" breaths.

4. Some have found it helpful is to do progressive muscle relaxation work to prepare their body, focusing on relaxing one part of your body at a time.

5. Close your eyes or focus on a calming picture (though for some people, closing your eyes is distracting or puts you to sleep).

6. Set a timer and focus on your breathing, a phrase, or a scripture for a few minutes.

She has seen her clients recover a sense of calm and let go of stress as they start intentionally focusing on relaxation.

Several resources provide more relaxation and mindfulness exercises like these. We personally love going to our yoga class. Traditionally, yoga prepares the body for meditation by focusing on breathing and releasing tension. At the end of the group meditation, yoga instructors often end with the saying "Namaste." Our yoga instructor translates this as "I honor the light within you." Others have translated this as "I bow to the divine within you." Guided online meditations by meditation gurus such as Deepak Chopra may help you focus on clearing your mind and connecting to your spiritual nature.[13] For example, on YouTube one meditation called "Living Carefree" starts with a discussion about avoiding the anxious refrain of "never enough" in our society and focusing on the refrain "I move through my days lighthearted and carefree, knowing all is well."[14] Relaxation apps for smartphones have multiplied in the last several years. One of our favorites is the app Calm, which provides daily mindfulness exercises, sleep stories, and masterclasses on mindful living. Many of these resources are spiritual in nature, and there are many gurus who teach from their own religious traditions. Thich Nahat Hanh is a Vietnamese monk and author who shares simple meditations in his books and also explores connections between Buddhism and Christianity.[15]

We have found that the practice of meditation fits well with many of our core beliefs as Latter-day Saint women—for example, doctrine that teaches us that we are spiritual beings and that the body is tied to our spirits.[16] The idea of divine nature has been taught to us from the time we were in young women and references to nurturing the light within are found throughout the scriptures. When Jen was a young girl, her mother taught her a powerful lesson on the power of visualizing light. Jen was horribly afraid of the dark. She saw shapes in her closet that looked like wolves, she pictured creatures under her bed, and the few times she saw a scary movie she imagined the hideous creatures walking down her very own street, getting closer to her house. Her mom taught her to visualize the light of Christ surrounding her, which became a protective practice for her as a child. She would think of the image of Christ in a painting of Him at the Second

13. https://www.deepakchopra.com
14. Chopra. (5 Jun 2014). Living Carefree—A Meditation with Deepak Chopra. *YouTube.* https://www.youtube.com/watch?v=XSNpGyG2jSw.
15. *Plum Village.* https://plumvillage.org/about/thich-nhat-hanh/.
16. D&C 88:15

Coming and imagine that light surrounding Him also surrounded her, and then she could fall asleep.

In the Doctrine and Covenants, there are some particularly beautiful passages about light. In 88:11–13, we read:

And the light which shineth, which giveth you light, is through him who enlighteneth your eyes, which is the same light that quickeneth your understandings;

Which light proceedeth forth from the presence of God to fill the immensity of space—

The light which is in all things, which giveth life to all things . . ..

Rather than being a spiritual distraction, practicing meditation has helped us nurture our spiritual beings and connect to our divine nature in our busy, hurried lives as mothers. In turn, we feel like it's easier to listen, to be patient, to nurture, and to serve if we are centered and calm.

One mother we know had a regular practice of doing yoga on Saturday mornings. When her daughter began struggling with anxiety, her daughter's therapist suggested yoga. The mother invited her to come to yoga, and it became a fun, shared experience that helped them both practice letting go of stress and tension. One of their favorite experiences was going on a family vacation and doing yoga on the beach with the waves rolling in below. It was a time of calm and peacefulness in a stormy year.

A regular practice of simple mindfulness exercises like these has been shown to have great benefits, including decreased stress, depression, anxiety, drug and alcohol abuse, and unhealthy eating.[11] For example, in an extraordinary series of studies, Buddhist monks came to the University of Wisconsin to help uncover the effects that practicing mindfulness had on the brain. The results of these studies are described in *Buddha's Brain* by Rick Hanson.[5] One of the studies found that when the monks meditated, generating a deep sense of calm and peace, their prefrontal cortex was in sync with other areas of the brain. Brain imaging research has also shown that blood flows to the prefrontal cortex during meditation[11]—as the prefrontal cortex is activated, creativity, planning, strategic self-control, and problem-solving are more likely as a result of meditation. Meditation may also prepare us for more meaningful prayer.

PRAYER

Like meditation, prayer is most effective when it is practiced daily. A popular analogy among Sunday school and seminary teachers is toothbrushing. Brushing everyday benefits the gums, prevents cavities, and provides a regular, minty fresh sensation. Caring for your teeth has even been linked with reduced heart disease, diabetes, and dementia.[17] But if you instead decide to brush for an hour once a week, you don't get the same benefits. In line with the idea of building habits, remembering daily prayer may be easier if it is tied to a daily habit that is already in place. For example, if you make your bed every day, the sight of an unmade bed can become a cue to kneel and pray before heading out the door. As parents, we are often shooting up mini prayers throughout the day:

- Please help Maya on her test today.
- Please guide me in helping Jack respond to the bullies at lunch time.
- Please help me figure out how to respond to the edgy outfit that José wore today.
- Thank you for an evening where chores actually went smoothly tonight.

However, we need the centering practice of communing in the morning, seeking revelation for the day. We also need the evening practice of reviewing the day, focusing on gratitude and the things that went well.

In a small book called *Letters to a Young Mormon,* with a touch of humor Adam Miller points out that one of the basics of prayer is staying awake! It's natural for our mind to wander, and Miller says, "The substance of prayer is this willingness to remember, to heave your wandering mind back, once more, in the direction of God, and then, when it drifts off yet again, to heave it still another time. To pray is to practice remembering God."[18] In other words, prayer is a daily practice that teaches on a microscale that beautiful Old Testament

---

17. Oral health; A window to your overall health. *Mayo Clinic: Healthy Lifestyle, Adult Health.* (4 Jun 2019). https://www.mayoclinic.org/healthy-lifestyle/adult-health/in-depth/dental/art-20047475.
18. Miller, A. S. (2014). *Letters to a Young Mormon.* Maxwell Institute Publications.

principle of "*teshuvah*" or returning to God. As we pray, every time our minds wander, we gently remind ourselves to turn back to Him.

As President Nelson reminded us, another principle of prayer is the practice of listening. To receive personal revelation, we need to listen. But what if the heavens don't open? What if no message comes? President Packer used the scripture-based metaphor of a candle to describe times when the Lord asks us to step into the dark and walk by faith. He said, "Somewhere in your quest for spiritual knowledge, there is that 'leap of faith,' as the philosophers call it. It is the moment when you have gone to the edge of the light and stepped into the darkness to discover that the way is lighted ahead for just a footstep or two. 'The spirit of man,' is as the scripture says, indeed 'is the candle of the Lord.'"[19]

Jen went through a period of time when she had a hard time feeling anything when she prayed, and it wasn't a few weeks or months—it was a couple of years. She remembers, "During this time, even though I prayed daily and read my scriptures, it felt like the heavens were silent. I couldn't feel the Spirit. Maybe the stress and burnout in my life was blocking spiritual pathways. Occasionally, a piece of music—like the hymn 'I Stand all Amazed'—would get through the spiritual blockade and tears would flow. The song I was most drawn to was 'A Child's Prayer' with its honest question, 'Heavenly Father, are you really there?' With time and healing, as I continued my daily spiritual habits and had opportunities to serve, I found reserves of spiritual strength in myself, and the Spirit started to flow freely again in my life."

When the heavens are silent, we may feel alone or abandoned. However, Adam Miller teaches youth a beautiful way to frame the experience of silence from the heavens. He says, "You may discover that God's silence is not itself a rebuke but an invitation. The heavens aren't empty, they're quiet. And God, rather than turning you away, may be inviting you to share this silence with him."[18] In other words, trusting that God is there with you brings peace. However, Jessica has learned from her clinical experience that when some people experience depression, they are numb to the Spirit and to many other emotions.

---

19. Packer, B. K. (Jan. 1983). The Candle of the Lord. *Ensign*.

When it's hard to feel peace, despite daily practice, reaching out to a therapist may be beneficial.

Few researchers have studied the impact of prayer. One has looked at the power of prayer in couple relationships and found that prayer strengthens couples, specifically the person praying tends to have greater relationship satisfaction, perhaps because it gives them a longer-term perspective.[20] We don't know of any research on this particular process of prayer that benefits parents and their children, but we suspect that a similar process is at play. Research has documented benefits of prayer as a larger practice of faith and religious community for parents and children.[7]

Certainly, the words of modern and ancient prophets testify of the power of prayer. Elder Holland instructed parents to pray for their children. He asked us, "Have our children ever unexpectedly opened a closed door and found us on our knees in prayer? Have they heard us not only pray *with* them but also pray *for* them out of nothing more than sheer parental love?"[21] Christ himself gave us the example of praying for children in their presence. The record in 3 Nephi 17 notes that "he took their little children, one by one, and blessed them, and prayed unto the Father for them."[22] The power of this experience lasted for generations.

The scriptures provide powerful examples of what a parent's prayer can do to bless their children. As we become parents of adolescents and young adults, we come to rely on prayer more fully as we let them exercise their own agency. As President Nelson taught parents several years ago, "Our privilege is to love them, to lead them, and to let them go."[23] Alma, the father, must have accessed the depths of his love as he poured out his heart in prayer for his son, who was on a destructive

---

20. Fincham, F. D., Beach, S. R., Lambert, N., Stillman, T., & Braithwaite, S. (2008). Spiritual behaviors and relationship satisfaction: A critical analysis of the role of prayer. *Journal of social and clinical psychology*, *27*(4), 362–388.
Fincham, F. D., & Beach, S. R. (2014). I say a little prayer for you: Praying for partner increases commitment in romantic relationships. *Journal of Family Psychology*, *28*(5), 587–593

21. Holland, J. R. (2003). A Prayer for the Children. General Conference, Apr.

22. 3 Nephi 17:21

23. Nelson, R. M. (1991). Listen to Learn. General Conference, Apr.

path. His example illustrates that God sends angels when parents pray for their children.[24]

When parents don't know what to do in a given parenting situation, prayer can be a powerful parenting tool. We offer a process of handling challenging parenting situations that we have found helpful. First, counsel together as parents or with other family members/leaders as appropriate. Jen and her husband Matthew often joke that if they are starting a project, if you add their two estimates on the cost or time it will take to complete and then divide by two, you will get a much better estimate. The same thing is true of our parenting—balancing both of our perspectives and ideas brings us closer to a successful solution. Next, we strategize on how to approach our child. For serious matters, we often approach him or her together.

Here is an example of the planned structure of a weekly conversation about screen time.

- Start by listing positives—things our child is doing well.
- Ask for their perspective on the situation.
- We bring up the things that we are concerned about and talk about balance.
- We give consequences or warnings as needed.
- We conclude with love and positive affirmations.

Then, after counseling together on our plan, we pray and listen for guidance. Sometimes we adjust our framing for the conversation after praying—for example, we may have a prompting that the conversation should be brought up casually by one of us when the moment feels right rather than formally together. Often, we feel good about our plan and move forward.

Here, we want to pause a moment and emphasize that this process of counseling works with other trusted confidants as well. For parents who are on their own, a trusted bishop, a brother or sister who regularly ministers to your family, or a friend who will brainstorm with you and respect your privacy can be an invaluable resource to work through challenging parenting moments. Ultimately, we each have the resource of a wise, all-knowing Father in Heaven, and a regular

---

24. Mosiah 27:14

practice of counseling with Him about parenting encourages the habit of measured, mindful reflection rather than hasty, fear-based reactions when we are worried about our kids.

CONNECTING WITH GOD IN NATURE

Another mindful practice is spending time in nature. Maybe it shouldn't surprise us that many of the prophets had spiritual experiences when they were surrounded by nature. Joseph Smith experienced the First Vision early in the morning in a grove of trees. Moses encountered the burning bush and received the ten commandments on the top of a mountain. Nephi's vision was filled with references to nature—wilderness, the tree of life, and a river. Our Savior Himself often taught in natural settings—the Sermon on the Mount and in the middle of the Sea of Galilee. One of the things nature does for us is give us perspective.

The awe, perspective, and grandeur of creation can take the edge off our anxiety-filled lives because it helps us understand that we are a part of something bigger than ourselves. We literally can see farther when we stand on the shore of an ocean or on the top of a mountain. Perhaps this is why President Kimball and President Eyring were willing to pray for "mountains to climb," knowing that challenge and adversity allow us to grow and see life more clearly.[25] One youth had a spiritual experience where he didn't necessarily expect it—out four-wheeling with his cousins and uncles at a family reunion. They had a break down deep into the Black Hills in South Dakota where the cell phone reception was spotty at best. They managed to get one or two texts out to the rest of the family, and then said a prayer trying to decide what to do. It was late in the afternoon, and they decided to hike straight down the hill off the path rather than going the long, round-about trail to try to get closer to the main road. In the meantime, family members had set off into the wilderness in an SUV to try to find them, guided by their last known location sent in a text. The boys emerged from tall grass and thickets right at the time that the family members were coming down

---

25. Eyring, H. B. (2012). Mountains to Climb. General Conference, Apr.

one of the many winding dirt paths in the hills. If they had come out onto the road ten minutes earlier or later, it would have been hours and maybe even days before they would have been found. This youth has shared his experience of family, nature, challenge, and an answer to prayer several times since then.

Scholars have also discussed the benefits of children spending time in nature from a health perspective. One book spurred a national conversation: *Last child in the woods: Saving our children from nature deficit disorder.*[26] The premise of the book is that we are biologically wired to be outdoors—for thousands of years our ancestors were focused on hunting, gathering, tending flocks, or farming. Our bodies are optimized for those contexts, but today, our children are expected to sit for 6–8 hours a day in school and then are enticed into virtual worlds once they get home. Often, screen entertainment seems more engaging to our youth than being outdoors. However, the research suggests that too much time on screens may be related to depression, anxiety, and insomnia.[27] A recent Common Sense Media survey found that children between 8 and 12 are spending nearly 5 hours a day on screens and teens are spending over 7 hours a day on screens, not including online homework.[28] Planning rich experiences in nature or outdoors as a family or youth program can help bring balance to digital consumption and give youth the opportunity to disconnect with screens and develop the habit of being in creation.

---

26. Louv, R. (2008). *Last child in the woods: Saving our children from nature-deficit disorder.* Algonquin books.

27. Twenge, J. M., Joiner, T. E., Rogers, M. L., & Martin, G. N. (2018). Increases in depressive symptoms, suicide-related outcomes, and suicide rates among US adolescents after 2010 and links to increased new media screen time. *Clinical Psychological Science, 6*(1), 3–17.

Li, X. S., Buxton, O. M., Lee, S., Chang, A., Berger, L. M., & Hale, L. (2018). 0803 Insomnia symptoms and sleep duration mediate the association between adolescent screen time and depressive symptoms. *Sleep, 41*, A298.

See also a good argument that reducing screen time won't solve mental health issues our youth are experiencing: Coyne, S. M. (11 Feb. 2020). Why reducing screen time won't fix the mental health crisis. *Psychology Today.* https://www.psychologytoday.com/us/blog/the-right-media-mindset/202002/why-reducing-screen-time-won-t-fix-the-mental-health-crisis

28. Common Sense Media. (2020). The Common Sense Census: Media use by Tweens and Teens, 2019. https://www.commonsensemedia.org/research/the-common-sense-census-media-use-by-tweens-and-teens-2019

CHAPTER 8

Resilience through Self-Compassion and Connecting with Others

When we decided to write about parenting and resilience, we were cautious because we know parenting is a sensitive area. So many of us carry "mom guilt" and—though it's not talked about a lot in our society—"dad guilt." We intentionally focused on patience to remind parents to be compassionate with ourselves as we all navigate this very messy process of parenting. No matter how much we learn about parenting, or even how much experience we have, each child and each situation is different. Patience in learning to be resilient is difficult, but when we approach the process with self-compassion, we are simultaneously learning and teaching our children. When the Savior presented the two greatest commandments, He could have simply said to love God and love others, but He included in the commandment the guidance to love others as we love ourselves.[1] When we are grounded in the love of God and self-compassion, we have a solid foundation on which to serve and love others.

---

1. Matthew 22:39

Having an eternal perspective is a key strategy to practicing self-compassion. Jessica was recently in Norway and decided to go on a hike/climb that was a bit more than she bargained for. There was a Polish man who kindly walked with her for a while and spoke in the bit of English he knew. When she was discouraged with the climb and said, "This is a long hike," he replied, "It's not long if you love the mountain." This insight could be applied to many things, but in the context of this book, if we focus on the love we have for our children and on the "mountain" or goal of returning to Heavenly Father together, we can have greater peace now. If we focus on our failures, our struggles to connect, our child's personality traits that get under our skin or imperfections, it becomes difficult to love and enjoy them. We need to be both compassionate and forgiving with our children and with ourselves. There are times when your shoe is stuck in the mud, ice makes you slip, and fear of falling makes the view on top of a mountain difficult to enjoy. In this chapter, we discuss self-care, practicing "mind over mood,"[2] and the goal of thriving rather than just surviving.

SELF-CARE

Women in particular are taught in our society to sacrifice for others. Think of the stories we learn as children. In *The Little Engine that Could*, several strong engines pass by the opportunity to help the dolls and toys so they could get to the other side of the mountain for the children. Finally, a female engine stops and pushes herself with mental coaching past her normal capacity to complete the task. In *Charlotte's Web*, the spider makes an extraordinary sacrifice that she knows will be her last in order to save Wilbur's life. In *The Giving Tree*, the female tree gives everything to the boy she loves, her apples, her branches and leaves, and her trunk, until she is just a stump. These are stories many of us cherished as a child and still love, but as we begin to think carefully about the role of mothering and burnout in parenting, we can see an unhealthy side to these stories—the theme of giving without renewal.

---

2. Greenberger, D. & Padesky, C.A. (1995). *Mind over Mood: a cognitive therapy treatment manual for clients.* Guilford press.

Christ's plan is not for us to give everything until we have nothing left to give, an empty shell of our former ability to bear fruit. In fact, in the scriptures, the symbolism of trees conveys a sense of renewal, nurturing, and life-giving power. In Alma 32:41–42, the prophet teaches, "If ye will nourish the word, yea, nourish the tree as it beginneth to grow, by your faith with great diligence, and with patience, looking forward to the fruit thereof, it shall take root; and behold it shall be a tree springing up unto everlasting life . . . and ye shall feast upon this fruit even until ye are filled, that ye hunger not, neither shall ye thirst." In Revelation, John describes the path leading to the throne of God, "and on each side of the river, was there the tree of life, which bare twelve manner of fruits, and yielded her fruit every month: and the leaves of the tree were for the healing of the nations."[3] As the master of the vineyard, the Savior is always willing to work with us, nurturing us to help us be healthy, to be able to share good fruit rather than bitter fruit.[4]

In the story of Martha and Mary, Martha's service wasn't the problem—in fact, Camille Olson points out that Christ had just told the story of the Good Samaritan, a story all about service.[5] But the fact that she was "cumbered about" and a bit resentful was the issue. Christ teaches her a gentle lesson about the "one thing that is needful," stopping to rest and find renewal at the Savior's feet.

Therapists often prescribe self-care as part of therapeutic healing, something we should engage in often. It is helpful for teens, and it is helpful for parents. We want to distinguish here between self-care and selfishness. Merriam Webster defines selfishness as, "a concern for one's own welfare or advantage at the expense of or in disregard of others: excessive interest in oneself." What we are talking about is a *balance* between taking care of ourselves and others instead of denying our own needs, so that we can find renewal and sustain our investment in relationships. When Jessica is teaching clients about self-care, she often encourages them to think about their senses. If you change one of your senses, you can change your environment. For example,

---

3. Revelation 22:2
4. Jacob 5
5. Olson, C. (Apr. 2019). Martha and Mary. *Ensign.*

listening to music that soothes you (hearing), lighting a candle (smell), getting a massage or taking a bath (touch), eating something you enjoy (taste), and looking at a picture that brings you peace (sight). She shares, "I encourage people to create a list of things or a basket of items and keep them handy. One of the things in my personal basket is a list of quotes from general authorities, scriptures, and favorite books. I enjoy fresh flowers when I'm struggling, and I appreciate a good cup of hot chocolate while listening to the Carpenters."

Other self-care suggestions include: getting a physical (especially if you are chronically struggling—be honest with your doctor), talking to friends, making long-term goals, trying yoga, taking time to be outside if possible, trying a new hobby, reading a book, or writing in a journal and reading it over (with the latest technology, making a password protected document on your computer can help you feel secure). In a moment of stress, it can be helpful to do a quick check in: When was the last time you ate a healthy meal sitting down? How much sleep did you get last night? Are there any hormonal patterns influencing you or your teen? When chronic stress seems to be weighing on you, it is helpful to look at the patterns you are creating in your life. Are you getting 7 to 8 hours of sleep, eating well, and asking for the support you need? Do you need to ask someone for help (from the Elders Quorum president or a friend) or get professional counseling? When we are taking care of ourselves, we are more able to give of ourselves, choose meaningful sacrifices and serve with a sense of renewal and love. We are more likely to develop a healthy pattern of connecting with others that influences our children to seek healthy connections. As Elder Holland said, "Fatigue is the common enemy of us all—so slow down, rest up, replenish, and refill."[6]

SELF-CARE THROUGH CONNECTING

There are times when we fear our children's weaknesses will define them or us, we feel overwhelmed with responsibilities that seem more than we can bear, and we are worried our efforts are insufficient.

6. Holland, J. R. (2013.) Like a Broken Vessel. General Conference, Oct.

During those times, we need to reach for connection—connection with our children, connection with parents "who know," and connection with our God who knows all our sorrows, pains, and weaknesses.

Referring to the mothers of the stripling warriors who taught their sons courage, truth, and obedience,[7] Julie Beck wrote about "mothers who know" and take to heart their responsibility to raise their children.[8] This could really apply to fathers who know as well, but here we focus on mothers in part because we are speaking from our own personal experience as moms. When seeking connection with mothers "who know," it is important to find women who are honest with you and keep your confidences. Also, finding women who offer you compassion without talking poorly about your beliefs or your family is essential. If the group of friends you are currently in struggles to support you and be compassionate and you can't seem to change the tide, then expanding your group by adding people or finding other groups can help you feel better about your mothering role. Jessica has found that doing things she loves introduces her to women who also love the same things. When ministering with her sisters, they share a love of the gospel. Volunteering at a horse barn introduced her to women who love horses and nature. Joining a book club she was able to normalize some of her experiences with her children and life as they discussed books they love. Working in a field she loves introduced her to dear people from many walks of life. Doing yoga also introduced her to women seeking peaceful meditation.

As noted in Chapter 3, social support is beneficial to our health, and evidence suggests that having a supportive friend may also help us parent more effectively. In one study, mothers were invited into a lab to complete a problem-solving task. When a friend was in the room supporting them, they were significantly more efficient problem solvers.[9] New mothers reported finding social support online,[10] though some interactions online were stressful. Other studies found

---

7. Alma 56:48
8. Beck, J. B. (2007). Mothers Who Know. General Conference, Oct.
9. DeGarmo, D. S., & Forgatch, M. S. (1997). Determinants of observed confidant support for divorced mothers. *Journal of Personality and Social Psychology*, *72*(2), 336–345.
10. Drentea, P., & Moren-Cross, J. L. (2005). Social capital and social support on the web: the case of an internet mother site. *Sociology of health & illness*, *27*(7), 920–943.

that activities were beneficial: blogging was associated with feeling connected[11] or connecting on social media was linked with low levels of depression.[12] The key here is to pay attention to whether the interactions are truly supportive.

When seeking connection with our children, it is important to connect on matters important to them. Julie Beck encourages "mothers who know" to spend time with their children. When Jessica's children were small, she was able to go to the park, zoo, or climbing wall to meet others who were trying to provide similar experiences to their children. Now that her children are a little older, it is more difficult to engage with parents of school-age children or teenagers. The best way she has found to meet mothers of similar-aged children is to do activities she and her children enjoy together and meet people together. For a time that was rock climbing, during another period it was a family gym where they swam together, and for a while bike riding as a family was common. Hiking as a family has been a passion, animals and the zoo, rollerblading, and currently they serve rescue horses together (children and adults lose interest in activities, so being flexible is important). Also, not making huge "to do lists" is also key. If you stress yourself or your child out trying to do everything you are both interested in, you might feel overwhelmed and less connected. It is more important that you are both enjoying something and that you are neither on the sidelines or the only one front and center.

Another way to connect with others is to connect with our ancestors and past. Jessica was recently at a Jewish Mental Health conference in Minneapolis. A singing group, Shir, sang a hymn with the words, "You are the vision that your grandmother prayed for. You are the dream that your grandfather dreamed." Connecting spirituality through generations is powerful. Helping youth see the intergenerational spiritual connections can help them feel less isolated. Lisa Miller, the author of *The Spiritual Child*, refers to the sacredness of

---

11. McDaniel, B. T., Coyne, S. M., & Holmes, E. K. (2012). New mothers and media use: Associations between blogging, social networking, and maternal well-being. *Maternal and child health journal, 16*(7), 1509–1517.

12. Miyata, K. (2002). Social support for Japanese mothers online and offline. *The internet in everyday life*, 520–548.

family across generations as a "field of love," a core asset for children as they develop.[13]

Hearing the specific things their own "people" have endured helps normalize current suffering.[14] Jessica shares, "When I am looking through family history and inevitably see children who pass at a young age, I think of my own miscarriage. I have told my daughters and nieces about a great, great, great grandmother who stood up to Union soldiers. I had ancestors who tried to homestead in the late fall on land in Tennessee only to awake to spring and realize their home was built on a pit of snakes. My children will not homestead on snakes, but they will have the experience of expecting a situation to turn out one way, only to have their vision turned upside down. Hopefully they will not need to face soldiers, but they will need courage to face many other things. Knowing that courage is part of their heritage may give them courage to face 21st century struggles. One of my favorite things to say about my ancestors to my children is 'that is the stuff you are made of.'" Knowing and sharing family history creates connectedness.

SERVING

Serving meals at shelters, helping at a hospital or places where children their age are vulnerable, working with animals, helping refugees, or seeing ministry assignments as a family assignment can help youth feel love and compassion for others. Serving helps children to understand people who are different from them. When youth see the struggles of others, it helps them to normalize their own struggles. One of the things youth struggle with the most is belonging, feeling like they don't fit in. Elder Gong reminds us, "Our campfire of faith can encourage us to minister in new, higher, and holier Spirit-filled ways. Such ministering brings miracles and the blessings of covenant belonging—where we feel God's love and seek to minister to others in

---

13. Miller, L. (2016). *The spiritual child: The new science on parenting for health and lifelong thriving*. New York: Macmillan.

14. An important note here. Some suffering should not be normalized. Racism and abuse are two examples of intergenerational suffering that we as individuals, communities, and society should be working to interrupt.

that spirit."[15] Patterns of service in our family life can teach youth to focus on helping others belong, and in the process, help them to feel that they belong.

Research has demonstrated that a positive approach to parenting makes a difference in teens volunteering to do service or help out, also known as "prosocial behavior." According to one study, parent's involvement with their kids and connection with them was linked to empathy and self-control.[16] In turn, teens who were empathetic and showed self-control were more likely to help strangers and be intentionally kind to their friends.[17] In a research project that Jen was involved with, feeling connected with parents was associated with positive experiences mentoring youth in the community, in part because a good parent-child relationship lead to empathy and positive attitudes.[18] As parents, one of the best things we can do to encourage prosocial behavior is to build a warm, communicative relationship with our teens.

CONSIDERING SACRIFICES

Sometimes in the Church, we have had the cultural notion that if something is a sacrifice then it must be what we should do. However, one of the things President Nelson has focused on recently is the idea of priorities[19]—we can't do it all, and really we shouldn't try. In Elder Oaks classic talk, "Good, Better, Best," he counseled, "We should begin by recognizing the reality that just because something is *good* is not a sufficient reason for doing it. The number of good things we can do far exceeds the time available to accomplish them. Some things

15. Gong, G. W. (2018). Our Campfire of Faith. General Conference, Oct.
16. Padilla-Walker, L. M., & Christensen, K. J. (2011). Empathy and self-regulation as mediators between parenting and adolescents' prosocial behavior toward strangers, friends, and family. *Journal of Research on Adolescence*, *21*(3), 545–551.
17. Padilla-Walker, L. M., & Christensen, K. J. (2011). Empathy and self-regulation as mediators between parenting and adolescents' prosocial behavior toward strangers, friends, and family. *Journal of Research on Adolescence*, *21*(3), 545–551.
18. Doty, J. L., Weiler, L. M., Mehus, C. J., & McMorris, B. J. (2019). Young mentors' relationship capacity: Parent–child connectedness, attitudes toward mentees, empathy, and perceived match quality. *Journal of Social and Personal Relationships*, *36*(2), 642–658.
19. Nelson, R. M. (2019). Spiritual Treasures. General Conference, Oct.

are better than good, and these are the things that should command priority attention in our lives."[20]

When we are faced with a decision to take on a new responsibility, which would require sacrifice, some principles of time management and family counseling may be helpful. We have found the following valuable guidelines in making decisions about when to make a sacrifice:

1. The time-honored object lesson of the rocks, pebbles, and sand filling a glass Mason jar applies. If we put in the sand first, the rocks and pebbles will never fit. But if we put in the two or three larger rocks, and then the pebbles and fill in with the sand, it's possible to get all three to fit. In the book *Deep Work,* Cal Newport advocates for identifying the 2 to 3 things in our life that matter most and organizing our time around those priorities.[21]

2. Sometimes we get an assignment or a calling, and we think we need to do it all on our own. Consider asking for assistance, formally or informally. At church, often we can ask specialists to pitch in for a onetime event. At home, this might mean making a call to a ministering sister or a neighbor and asking for a favor.

3. Letting some things go. Maybe the lawn doesn't get mowed this week. Maybe we don't make the handouts for a lesson we had planned to. Maybe our visit to someone becomes a phone call. Maybe we order online rather than shop in person. Maybe we decline to become head coach or turn down an offer to speak in another city.

4. When we are asked to take a calling, we can counsel with the bishopric and give them the context of our family situation. A lesson Jen learned on her mission came from the mission president. He encouraged her to talk to him about what was really going on in an area—she had assumed that he would

20. Oaks, D. H. (2007). Good, Better, Best. General Conference, Oct.
21. Newport, C. (2016). *Deep work: Rules for focused success in a distracted world.* Hachette, UK.

just be inspired to make a change if needed, but the mission president explained that it helped him to get her perspective on the situation.

5. Counseling with your family is another critical principle. As families, we are all connected—like a mobile that hangs above a baby's crib, if you pull on one member, every other member is affected. When one member of the family makes a sacrifice, often all the other members are affected by that sacrifice. Getting everyone's input and understanding the pros and cons from everyone's perspective can go a long way toward weathering the challenges that come with sacrifice.

Ultimately, our hope is to align our will with Heavenly Father's will. In a recent talk, President Nelson counseled:

As you shift your focus away from worldly distractions, some things that seem important to you now will recede in priority. You will need to say no to some things, even though they may seem harmless. As you embark upon and continue this lifelong process of consecrating your life to the Lord, the changes in your perspective, feelings, and spiritual strength will amaze you![203]

Another skill that helps us decide where to put our energy is setting personal boundaries. In part, this may include learning to say no or setting up boundaries to limit time spent in unhealthy relationships. For example, years ago a young father lost his sister in a tragic way. At the time, he was the ward mission leader. Shortly after her death, he attended a ward council meeting where he was asked to report on why he hadn't accomplished his assignments. Looking back, the father realized that he probably didn't need to return to ward council quite so quickly. Taking time to mourn and heal would have been absolutely appropriate. He also could have set expectations with the bishop before going back to join the ward council by letting him know that he was struggling. Another example is setting boundaries with individuals who require constant attention or who constantly share negative energy. If we have a friend who constantly complains or lays on thick sarcasm, we might think carefully about how often we spend time with them and how we feel afterwards. It might be appropriate to limit our time with them if we feel drained after our visits. It might be appropriate to prayerfully and gently suggest getting professional help. It may be a signal that our own reserves are low and that we need to find ways to give ourselves self-care in order to be there for our friend. There is no one right answer in this situation, but being aware of our own state of mind can help us successfully navigate setting helpful boundaries.

Helping children develop boundaries is also important. Some children come wired with firm boundaries. They make their needs known (loudly) from toddlerhood onward. If someone interferes with their toy, friend, or treat, everyone within earshot is fully aware. Others struggle to stand up for themselves and look to people around them for structure and reassurance. Teaching the child who easily sets boundaries to encourage and respect the boundaries of others while simultaneously encouraging the child who struggles with boundaries is essential. Recently, Jessica had an interaction with her children where one child who effortlessly establishes her presence was encouraged to see her brother's perspective. Her brother was given words and encouragement to express his own boundaries. Of course, the next disagreement wasn't handled perfectly—most of us are not wired to learn that quickly. If those patterns are created and encouraged over and over, by the time they both hit adulthood, they likely will have learned some life skills to use with other humans without changing their personalities to fit a certain mold. It's crucial not to shame one child for not responding like someone around them (you, a friend, or a sibling). We need all types of people in our lives and in the world.

COGNITIVE DISTORTIONS IN OUR RELATIONSHIPS WITH OTHERS

Cognitive distortions can get in the way of healthy relationships with others, and particularly in the context of parenting. What is a cognitive distortion? In short, these are biased habits in our thinking. In other words, we often reinforce beliefs in our minds that may have origins in truth but that we have exaggerated and colored by our thinking patterns or experiences. For example, I may feel inept at dealing with a particular child's struggle with getting their homework done in a patient manner. If the child refused to respond until I lose patience over and over again, the cycle may reinforce a cognitive distortion that my child only responds when I "lose it." We may then see others around us deal with their children patiently, and we generalize the distortion to create self-talk that "I am a bad parent." We sometimes try to repair faulty thinking to help ourselves and others to "feel better" by saying internally, "No, I'm a good parent." However, if I just blew up at my daughter, I don't believe the thought replacement and tend to feel worse.

Balanced thinking is more effective. In the book *Mind Over Mood,* the authors encourage us to acknowledge both sides of our feelings.[22] A balanced thought following a blow up might be "I'm struggling more with my temper with Suzy. Generally speaking, I feel better when my temper is under control, and last week when I could have yelled at Suzy, I walked away. I have the ability but not always the energy to maintain my temper." The line of thinking that both acknowledges our flaws and our strengths simultaneously is not only healthier, but also easier to swallow for our psyche. Your children don't need perfect parenting—they need *you*. Children couldn't handle having parents that did everything perfectly because they wouldn't be able to grapple with their own weaknesses. As we struggle with our own imperfections, we show our children how to manage difficulties and shortcomings.

Another cognitive distortion is the self-serving bias, our tendency to overestimate our contribution and underestimate others' contributions. When Jessica was teaching human behavior in the social environment for 7 years, she offered the same assignment every year. The students had to work in a group to do a presentation on a psychological theory. Prior to their presentation, she would teach the students about group dynamics and the roles that people play in groups. She then had them write their own paper reflecting on the group, the role they played, their own strengths and weaknesses in this group, how it related to other groups they were in and what they might use from

22. Greenberger, D., & Padesky, C. A. (1995). *Mind over Mood: a cognitive therapy treatment manual for clients.* Guilford press.

the experience in the future. Interestingly, each year about 75% of students were sure they alone led the group in effort and modeling. Even when this phenomenon was stated prior to writing the paper, it appeared to have no effect. This example seems to indicate that we either do not see all the roles we play in groups or sometimes we are unaware of the way we are perceived by others. The self-serving bias shows up in family life too—husbands and wives both tend to overestimate the amount of housework they do. Adolescents tend to be hyperaware of hypocrisy and simultaneously self-conscious. One thing we can do as parents is become aware of our own biases, admit our mistakes, and credit others. In doing so, we model humility and show our young people how to take a balanced approach to life and strengthen relationships by modeling evenhandedness.

COMPARING OURSELVES TO OTHERS

At times, we may find ourselves browsing Instagram or Facebook, comparing everyone else's seemingly perfect lives to our own. These issues affect us as parents as well as youth—we can start to address this by talking to youth and practicing together. It's unfair to ourselves that we compare our moments of weakness to everyone else's *seemingly* perfect lives. When we encourage healthy interaction in children, we don't want them all to be leaders; we aren't trying to make everyone the captain of everything or homecoming queen. Instead, we want to teach children to be resilient, teach them to connect with others, and teach them to be prepared for the hard times in life and seek joy and peace. It's easier said than done, though, when it appears that the homecoming king (and his mom) have everything you want for your family.

Recently, Jessica was talking to a friend about her vacation. She said something like "your pictures were gorgeous. It looked like such a tranquil place." Her friend then described the chaos that ensued before and after the picture. Jessica had been thinking, "We never have tranquil vacations," and wondering what she could do to create that kind of break for her family. Then she discovered her fellow parent hadn't figured it out either. As she thought more about this experience, it struck her that on that long, beautiful, arduous hike up the mountain in Norway, when she started the hike, she imagined the summit, the beautiful moments when she would look out over the valley and the sea and feel peace. Those moments happened in her six-and-a-half-hour journey, and she took pictures and reveled in the beauty of God's creations. However, other moments included: falling, blisters, her shoe stuck in mud, slipping, walking through icy water, getting lost, and feelings of discouragement. Sometimes sharing the discouraging side of things can help us realize that the pictures are only part of the full experience.

Jessica spoke with someone in the audience after presenting at a recent youth fireside about mental health and preparing for a mission. The woman stated that she wasn't sure one of her children could serve a mission because they were "introverted" and quiet. It struck Jessica that we often think of the "perfect missionary" as one who is athletic, beautiful, has a great smile, can talk to anyone, and was the captain of the football team, homecoming queen, etc. The ironic thing about that is if you look at investigators, they may not relate as well to that guy and might more easily relate to the young man who is a little introverted, likes to work on engines, plays a bit of videogames, and loves Marvel. God needs *all* of us in His kingdom. He needs our beautiful flaws, our challenges, and our strengths. We are unique on purpose. God created us to be different from one another and celebrating your individuality and your child's will bring you and them peace.

ACCEPTANCE

The crux of parenting may well be accepting our children for who they are as people and ourselves for the parent we are currently. This type of wholehearted acceptance is at the heart of the Savior's admonition to "Love your neighbor as yourself."[23] Even if we want/need to change, when we accept where we are on the path currently, it will grant us greater hope and compassion with ourselves for the future. One of Jessica's favorite sayings in a video from John Gottman's "love lab" teaching couples' therapists is that you can't take an Eeyore couple

---

23. Matthew 22:39

(e.g., low energy, etc.) and make them into a Tigger (e.g., bounding energy). When we look at a child that is content to stay home and enjoys reading and small groups and try to convince them they should "get out there" for every dance, every social experience that comes up at church, school, and in the community and expect they will become "Tiggerish," they may in fact feel overstimulated and anxious. Instead, encouraging our introverted child to get out there occasionally (so as to prepare for future stressors) and monitoring to make sure they get the time alone that they need may be more important. By the same token, for a very social child who struggles to want to read and be alone, constantly being told they "should" be staying home more can also create anxiety. In Jessica's work, she has seen it be more difficult when a parent is the opposite of the child. It can also be beneficial because each of you can learn from the other person's point of view.

Other times we cringe inside when our children don't represent the "ideal." One dear friend who has been a Relief Society president three times shared an experience where she was sitting in ward council, and someone asked, "Who is that guy who sits in the back with the messy hair?" At the time, her son, in his mid-twenties, had been taking his two little girls to church on his own. The bishop responded, "Sister, I think he's talking about your son." While she felt that cringe on the inside, she simply replied, "I'm just glad he's here." As parents, leaders, and fellow worshipers, sometimes we are overconcerned with outside appearances, and our inner critiques about others' choices don't go unnoticed by youth.

Self-compassion helps us to be mindful and nurturing as we experience negative emotions and are intentional about building positive attitudes and experiences. Elder Uchtdorf recently reminded us, "Discipleship is not about doing things perfectly; it's about doing things intentionally."[24] He continued by echoing Dumbledore, "It is your choices that show what you truly are, far more than your abilities."[25] The same can be said about parenting. When we have self-compassion, we are on solid ground to help others and nurture our

---

24. Uchtdorf, D. F. (2019). Your Great Adventure. General Conference, Oct.

25. Paraphrased from Rowling, J. K. (1998). *Harry Potter and the Chamber of Secrets.* Bloomsbury.

children. This is a lesson Jen learned in a poignant way as a senior in high school on spring break with some friends. Her parents were in the middle of a messy divorce, and this trip was a welcome escape. Even though she was not a strong swimmer, every day during the trip she swam out to a sandbar, sometimes on her own, sometimes with friends. One day, the swim was really challenging, and for a while, she honestly didn't know if she would make it. She finally got a foothold onto the sandbar and stood panting on the edge. When she saw her friends behind her also struggling to get to the sandbar, her first instinct was to reach out to them and give them a hand. But when she got too close to the edge, she started to lose her own footing and get dragged back into the water herself. She had to be on more solid ground to help others. Reflecting on the experience later that week, she realized that the situation was a metaphor for her life at the time—she really wanted to reach out and help her younger brothers, but she needed to intentionally work on healing and get on emotionally solid ground in order to be there for her family. Practicing patient resilience means being reflective, understanding and acknowledging our inner emotional life, finding balance between the push and pull of life, and leaning on our Savior to restore our soul.[26] As we parent with this sense of balance and attention to the state of our own soul, our children will learn to appreciate that goodness, mercy, and comfort can be found even in difficult times.

---

26. Psalm 23:3

EPILOGUE

Writing this book has been a journey. We've woven in lessons that we've learned from our professional lives—from research, from teaching, from doing therapy. At the same time, the hard lessons we've learned from making mistakes in our parenting over the last four years have made it into this book. Sometimes it's been tough to write, knowing that we are positioning ourselves as experts but at times feeling at a loss in our own parenting journey. At other times it's been therapeutic. We've shared with you many of the experiences, scriptures, talks, and insights that we have found inspirational during our own challenges parenting. It's been a humbling experience, and the idea of practicing patience has taken on new meaning.

One lesson we've learned writing this book is that we need each other. Neither one of us would have ever written the book alone, but together we shared our experiences with each other, talked about parenting, and thought about gospel principles that applied to parenting. We returned home and counseled with our partners about parenting challenges. We talked with other friends about the struggles they were having. Our families have different family cultures and traditions, and we were reminded of Sister Okazaki's talk "Baskets and Bottles." She asks, "Are we perfect in any of these things? No. We all have much to learn. Are we exactly the same in any of these things? No. We are all at different points on our journey back to our Father in Heaven."[1] She observes that we share the lifesaving, renewing doctrines of Christ's Atonement, but how we practice our faith may be different. In her words, "the packaging is optional."

She gives the example of a woman in Utah who canned fruit compared to a woman in Polynesia who gathered fruit in baskets. She says, "The basket and the bottle are different containers, but the content is the same: fruit for a family. Is the bottle right and the basket wrong? No, they are both right. They are containers appropriate to the culture and the needs of the people. And they are both appropriate for the content they carry, which is the fruit." Instead of comparing ourselves negatively to our neighbors or judging our neighbors, she reminds us to focus on cultivating the fruit of the Spirit found in Galatians 5:22–23, including "love, joy, peace, longsuffering, gentleness, goodness, faith, meekness, [and] temperance."

Parenting is a journey with ups and downs, and recently a friend who has watched one of her children suffer tremendously, who has struggled through self-blame and come to a place of peace, shared the wisdom she learned. Her joy (and she radiates it) is found in focusing on the Savior. Resilience means overcoming the hardest challenges in our lives to find joy, and ultimately this is what we want for our children. President Nelson put it beautifully: "The joy we feel has little to do with the circumstances of our lives and everything to do with the focus of our lives."[2]

One of our greatest takeaways after writing the book has been the idea that as parents one of the greatest gifts we can give our kids is to continue trying. In Elder Uchtdorf's words, "Even when you fail, you can choose not to give up, but rather discover your courage, press forward, and rise up. That is the great test of the journey. God knows that you are not perfect, that you will fail at times. God loves you no less when you struggle than when you triumph. Like a loving parent, He merely wants you to keep intentionally trying."[3] Notice the words "like a loving parent"? This is exactly what we are hoping to teach our

1. Okazaki, C. N. (1996). Baskets and Bottles. General Conference, Apr.
2. Nelson, R. M. (2016). Joy and Spiritual Survival. General Conference, Oct.
3. Uchtdorf, D. F. (2019). Your Great Adventure. General Conference, Oct.

children, and as usual our actions speak louder than our words. When we are able to rely on the Savior and bring Him our broken hearts, we are teaching our children to do the same, to find healing in His arms—and that is truly the essence of the gospel.

RESOURCES

MENTAL ILLNESS

National Alliance on Mental Illness
Phone: 800.950.NAMI (800.950.6264) (available 10 a.m. to 6 p.m., ET, weekdays)
People They Help: Individuals, families, professionals

SUICIDE PREVENTION

National Suicide Prevention Lifeline
Phone: 800.273.TALK (800.273.8255)
TTY: 800.799.4TTY (800.799.4889)
People They Help: Families, concerned individuals

YOUTH IN TROUBLE/RUNAWAYS

National Runaway Switchboard
Phone: 800.RUNAWAY (800.786.2929)
People They Help: Runaway and homeless youth, families

MEDIA GUIDANCE

Common Sense Media
https://www.commonsensemedia.org/
People They Help: Parents trying to make decisions about their children's media

ABOUT THE AUTHORS

Dr. Jennifer Doty

Dr. Jennifer Doty earned her doctorate from the University of Minnesota in Family Social Science with an emphasis on youth development and prevention. She has published over thirty scholarly articles, and her research is built around the idea that parent-child relationships are key leverage points for improving both parent and adolescent health and well-being. Integrating faith and science to support families is a central theme of her work. A native of Chicago, she now calls sunny Florida home. In her spare time, Dr. Doty enjoys field work with her own three teenage and young adult children.

Jessica Peterson

Jessica Peterson, LICSW, received her master's degree in social work in 1999 from Brigham Young University. She has provided services for families and children as a therapist in private practice and LDS Family Services, a behavior specialist, an adoption disruption clinician, a clinical director at a school for high-risk youth, and a clinician for veteran families. Jess teaches as an adjunct professor and has taught courses in couples, families, and human behavior in the social environment to clinical social work students.

Acknowledgments

Jennifer

I would like to acknowledge the women in my book club back in Minnesota and others who shared their parenting stories. They honestly shared their ups and downs and gave permission for us to include some of those stories in these pages.

Thank you to my mentors, who have spent hours giving me feedback on my writing.

Thank you to my brothers for taking my road trip calls: To Chris for connecting me with friends and the first opportunity to get some of these ideas out into the public. To Mike for sharing podcasts and books. And to Tom for giving car advice whenever needed.

I'm grateful to my mom for teaching me how to slow down and smell the roses, and to my dad for listening to me when I'm stressed out (which is more often than I like to admit).

I'm grateful to Claire, Haven, and Nate for giving me grace when I mess up parenting and for giving me permission and even encouragement to share our family stories in this book.

I'm lucky and blessed to have Matthew as a partner, who not just supports but also celebrates my goals and accomplishments as we parent and do family life side by side.

Finally, Jessica: This book would not have been written without your wholehearted friendship. I admire your zest for life and sense of adventure, your clinical wisdom and patient resilience, which all made it into the pages of this book.

Jessica

I am so thankful for friends who endure my constant busyness, curiosity, and desire for change. I'm thankful to be connected to friends from high school, college, our many moves, and current friends who keep me grounded, listen to my troubles, and are up for spontaneous fun (and books).

Thank you to my brother, Brigham. You are the best brother/cheerleader in the universe. Anything I'm excited to do I always hear, "How can I help or what can I do?" I feel very lucky to be your sister. Thanks Mom, you have dedicated your life to Brigham and I. We are lucky to be your kids. Dad, thanks for being a cheerleader for the book. I'm grateful for my children, Elizabeth, Ben, James, Sarah, and Taylor. I have learned so much from each of you and I appreciate your kindness when I fall short as a Mom. You are my favorite people to hang with. Jen, I can't believe what a gift you have been in my life. I'm thankful for your tenacity, curiosity, and courage. Thanks for never giving up on this book. Without you, it would just be random thoughts on a page.

We would like to acknowledge our early readers: thank you for all your time, efforts, and feedback. We are lucky to have friends and family willing to read and offer advice.

Thank you to our Hang In There community. We are grateful for the opportunity to learn from those willing to be interviewed and provide input.

AUTHORS
CEDAR FORT
Publishing & Media
WANTED

You've dreamed of accomplishing your publishing goal for ages—holding *that* book in your hands. We want to partner with you in bringing this dream to light.

Whether you're an aspiring author looking to publish your first book or a seasoned author who's been published before, we want to hear from you. Please submit your manuscript to

CEDARFORT.SUBMITTABLE.COM/SUBMIT

CEDAR FORT HAS PUBLISHED BOOKS IN THE FOLLOWING GENRES

- LDS Nonfiction
- General Nonfiction
- Fiction
- Cookbooks
- Juvenile & YA
- Children's Books
- Biographies
- Self-Help
- Regency Romances
- Comic & Activity books
- Cozy Mysteries
- Children's books with customizable character illustrations